THE WESTERN FRONTIER LIBRARY

THE LIFE OF
JOHN WESLEY HARDIN

For Tralley
Hewton
Slaten.

Joanna

989·1750·

JOHN WESLEY HARDIN

THE LIFE OF
John Wesley Hardin
As Written by Himself

—

WITH AN INTRODUCTION BY
ROBERT G. McCUBBIN

NORMAN AND LONDON

UNIVERSITY OF OKLAHOMA PRESS

Library of Congress Catalog Card Number: 61–6493

ISBN: 0–8061–1051–1

The Life of John Wesley Hardin as Written by Himself is Volume 16 in The Western Frontier Library.

10   11   12   13   14   15   16   17

CONTENTS

———

ILLUSTRATIONS

___

INTRODUCTION

———

THE ORIGINAL MANUSCRIPT of John Wesley Hardin's autobiography was discovered among his personal possessions shortly after his death at the hands of John Selman in El Paso, Texas, on August 19, 1895. A year later the book was published by a small country press known as Smith and Moore in the south central Texas town of Seguin, Guadalupe County. It was a paper-back book printed on a low-quality paper which quickly became yellowed and brittle. The original books were sold for fifty cents each, but today a copy would be fairly expensive as rare books go.

John Wesley Hardin has become somewhat of a legend in Texas. He ranks head and shoulders above other notable desperadoes of that state, which certainly had no scarcity of the breed. Ben Thompson, Bill Longley, Sam Bass, and King Fisher are not names to be scoffed at when calling the role of the desperadoes of the West, and they were all Texas products. These notables, along with hundreds of lesser-known "hard cases," kept the famed and efficient Texas Rangers busy for several decades following the Civil War.

Hardin was born on May 26, 1853, in Bonham, Fannin County, Texas, the son of James G. Hardin, a Methodist preacher of the frontier mold. The proud parents christened the baby with the name of the founder of their faith, John Wesley. As he grew up, the boy led the typical life of a frontier lad and received an average education for the time and place.

Texas was filled with bitter strife and hatred in the period during and immediately following the Civil War. It was a bad time to get in trouble with the law, as young Wes Hardin found out. His first serious trouble came when he shot a Negro who tried to bully him. In normal times his father would have made him surrender and stand trial, but the state was then ruled by Union military forces and the hated State Police of Reconstruction Governor Edmund J. Davis, composed almost entirely of freed Negroes. Therefore, at fifteen years of age, Wes Hardin became a fugitive. There followed a number of encounters with the law, and, while still only a lad, Hardin became known throughout the country for his daring and skill with weapons.

This book tells with vivid reality the rise of John Wesley Hardin's fame as the master gunfighter of Texas. It is an amazing story, sometimes almost unbelievable. In the ten years between his first killing in 1868 and his final capture and imprisonment in 1878, the outlaw killed more than a score of men in personal combat.

John Wesley Hardin's own account ends with his decision to study law while in prison at Huntsville. The incidents following his release are summed up briefly in an appendix composed of letters and newspaper clippings. The particulars concerning his death are well covered in the various news stories, and little can be added to these firsthand reports, but since there is not a complete account of Hardin's activities from the time he was released from prison until he was killed, a summary—as accurate as I can make it—follows.

Having cast aside the shackles of Rusk Prison, Hardin made a sincere effort to live an honest and trouble-free life. His wife, Jane, had died on November 6, 1892, more than a year before his release from prison on February 17, 1894. With his son and two daughters he first lived with an old friend, Fred Duderstadt, on his ranch near Gonzales, Texas. After a full pardon was granted on March 16, 1894, Wes and his children moved into Gonzales. There he led an exemplary life, attending church services regularly and making many friends. There he also applied for and passed an examination to practice law.

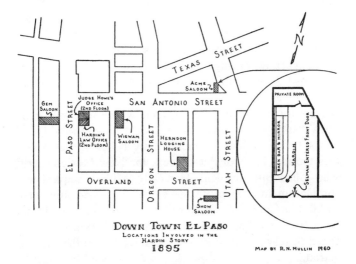

DOWN TOWN EL PASO
LOCATIONS INVOLVED IN THE HARDIN STORY
1895

MAP BY R. N. MULLIN 1960

Headstrong, with an uncontrollable temper, Hardin became involved in a controversial race for sheriff of Gonzales County. He was violently opposed to a candidate named W. E. Jones and made no bones about it. Not content to remain peaceably in the background, he wrote scorching letters concerning Jones and sent them to a local newspaper. He accused Jones of having had a hand in his escape from the Gonzales jail in 1872. Old and bitter feelings were aroused, and Hardin's name once more was spread across the whole of Texas. Despite the opposition, Jones won the election by a scant margin. Deeply disappointed, Hardin left Gonzales in November of 1894 and moved to the home of friends in Riddleville. Many believe it was at this time that he began work on his book.

In December, Wes opened a law office at Junction, Texas. In near-by London he was introduced to a young girl named Callie Lewis, whom he married on January 8, 1895, but the marriage did not last long. Callie Lewis, apparently the victim of infatuation for Hardin, left him shortly after the wedding and refused to see him again.

His marriage having failed, Hardin went to Kerrville and remained there for three months. In April he was asked to represent a relative as a lawyer. The request came from the notorious "Killing Jim" Miller, whose wife was Hardin's cousin. Miller was a scoundrel, a hired assassin, and had killed a number of men. Many believed that Miller was the real killer of Pat Garrett, the New Mexico sheriff who killed Billy the Kid. Ironically, Miller's request was for Hardin to help prosecute a man who had attempted to kill him, and not to help Miller out of a scrape. Hardin went to El Paso and took part in the trial. When the jury failed to reach a decision, the judge scheduled the case for retrial.

Hardin decided to remain in town until after the completion of the case and rented a room at Mrs. Williams' Herndon Lodging House. He opened a law office in a second-floor room on El Paso Street. In 1895, El Paso was one of the toughest towns in the country—Abilene, Tombstone, and Dodge City rolled into one. Old-timers assert that Hardin made a sincere effort to stay away from trouble during his first few weeks there, going out of his way to avoid gunplay. But eventually he began to frequent the saloons and gambling dens once again. He became a familiar figure at the Gem Saloon and Gambling Emporium, the Wigwam Saloon, the Acme Saloon, and Roy Barnum's Show Saloon.

It was at the Gem Saloon that Hardin was accused of holding up a faro game on April 16, 1895. He was arrested and appeared before Justice of the Peace Walter D. Howe. After paying a fine of $25.00, he was released. From this point, Hardin sank lower and lower. He took to keeping company with a Mrs. Helen Bulah M'Rose, and the two lived at the Herndon Lodging House. Finally, as he was standing at the Acme Saloon bar on August 19, 1895, old John Selman stepped through the swinging doors and shot him through the back of the head.

The El Paso police notified Fred Duderstadt of Hardin's death, and he advised Hardin's children not to attend the funeral. Shortly thereafter, John Wesley Hardin, Jr., traveled to El Paso to claim his father's personal effects. The owner of the house where Hardin had rented a room refused to release the dead man's trunk, and the services of an attorney were required before the property could be obtained.

Through the untiring efforts of Hon. P. S. Sowell, the Hardin manuscript was finally turned over to his children. The son read it and wanted to publish it at once, even though his sisters were reluctant. The book had been published only a few days when he decided to withdraw it from circulation. At that time nearly 2,500 copies were stored in a San Antonio warehouse. A flood later ravaged the warehouse and destroyed the books, or so the owner claimed; however, it was later learned that a number had been sold by the warehouse owner to a San Antonio bookstore prior to the flood. Many water-stained copies of the book are in existence today, evidently salvaged from the flooded warehouse.

Thus the book became a collector's item and brought a high price whenever a copy could be found. The San Antonio bookstore did not release its copies at once, but sold them one or two at a time at a price of $25.00 each. Later, when the store changed hands, four hundred copies were sold to a gun collector. In 1950, Ed Bartholomew of Ruidoso, New Mexico, bought these copies from the collector. Those copies which are scattered throughout many Texas bookstores apparently stem from the supply originally stored in the San Antonio warehouse.

Almost immediately after the book appeared, the cry went up that it was a forgery, that Hardin did not possess the necessary education and talent to write such a volume. Even up to the present time critics have expressed the same opinion. Burton Rascoe, in his *Belle Starr, the Bandit Queen* (New York, 1941), says, "This book, on the face of it, is a forgery; for John Wesley Hardin was almost illiterate and a murderous bandit by the time he was sixteen years old; and this book is written with expert literary skill." (Exception must be taken to Rascoe's statement that Hardin was a bandit. A dangerous, wanted badman, yes, but he was not a robber of stagecoaches or banks.) In his bibliography, *Six Guns and Saddle Leather* (Norman, 1954), Ramon Adams voiced a similar opinion: "The book is carefully written; in fact, so well written that it seems to have come from the pen of someone not so illiterate as Hardin."

Various facts indicate, however, that John Wesley Hardin was not as illiterate as might be expected. His schooling was that of the average youngster in post–Civil War days. He remained in school until he was fifteen years of age, at which time he committed his first offense against the law. In those days on the frontier it was rare for a young man to keep going to school after his fifteenth birthday. According to Hardin's own statement, he excelled in his studies and generally stood at the head of his class. With his parental background, it would seem natural that he should excel in scholastic endeavors. Even while a fugitive from the law, he went to Round Rock, Texas, with the intention of completing his studies. However, on account of the careful searching of the State Police, Hardin was forced to leave Round Rock and to continue his studies in hiding. Even so, he was able to pass satisfactorily his diploma examination on the pre-law subjects he had studied, and was graduated.

In prison, Hardin read the Bible and many books on theology. There he was appointed superintendent of the Sunday schools. Later he became more interested in the law than the ministry, his father's calling, and studied law during his remaining days in prison. After his release and ultimate pardon, he passed the examination for the bar in the state of Texas. The letters written by Hardin while he was in prison are obviously the work of an educated person.

These facts seem to indicate that Hardin was capable of writing the book just as it was published. Possibly portions of it were reworked by an editor, but basically, I believe, the book is as Hardin himself wrote it. There is no record that the original manuscript is still extant. No doubt the printer tossed it into the wastebasket after the type had been set up. However, there are still living relatives of Hardin who testify that they saw the manuscript in its original form.

Just when John Wesley Hardin began work on his autobiography is not known. While in the Huntsville prison he often wrote his wife that he planned such a book. He hinted that she would play a prominent role in the work, and that it would tell the world how unjustly he had been treated and how he had been forced into a life of killing to escape being killed. He asked his wife to keep his letters, and they are now in the possession of Hardin descendants. Not once did he mention that he had actually started to write this story of his life.

Lewis Nordyke, author of *John Wesley Hardin, Texas Gunman* (New York, 1957), believed that Hardin began work on it the latter part of 1894, some months after his release from prison. Hardin's first wife, who, as has been said, died the year before his release, faithfully kept all his letters to her. These, together with other notes and documents, Hardin carried safely in a trunk until his own death one and one-half years after leaving Huntsville.

An incident related by the late J. Marvin Hunter, of Bandera, Texas, seems to verify the fact that Hardin was working on his book at the time of his marriage to Miss Callie Lewis. In his *Album of Gunfighters* (with Noah H. Rose, San Antonio, 1951), Hunter says: "I met John Wesley Hardin at Mason, Texas, in the early part of the year 1895, when he came into the Mason *Herald* office to get an estimate on the cost of printing a small book, the story of his turbulent life. At that time Hardin was forty-two years old, about five feet ten inches in height, weighed about 160 pounds, and wore a heavy mustache. He was of light complexion and had mild blue eyes. A few days after he was in Mason he married a very young girl at London, twenty-five miles west of Mason." As Hunter's press was inadequate for producing a book, he was unable to give Hardin an estimate. The manuscript evidently was well on its way at that time or Hardin would not have been interested in printing costs.

Throughout the years writers have depended upon Wes Hardin's book for source material with apparently little or no attempt to check its accuracy. Adams' *Six Guns and Saddle Leather: A Bibliography of Books and Pamphlets on Western Outlaws and Gunmen* lists ninety-five entries concerning John Wesley Hardin. Most of the longer accounts depart very little from Hardin's autobiography. Thomas Ripley appears to have relied upon it heavily in his *They Died With Their Boots On* (New York, 1935), a book dealing with most of the notorious Texas gunmen and desperadoes. Interesting accounts about Hardin have appeared in other, kindred books: William MacLeod Raine's *Famous Sheriffs and Western Outlaws* (Garden City, N. Y., 1929); Eugene Cunningham's *Triggernometry* (New York, 1934); and books written by Owen P. White, including *Trigger Fingers* (New York, 1926) and *Lead and Likker* (New York, 1932). In 1953 the Frontier Press of Texas published *Kill or Be Killed,* by Ed Bartholomew, and the New American Library in 1956 brought out a biography of John Wesley Hardin entitled *The Fastest Gun in Texas,* by J. H. Plenn and C. J. LaRoche. The last contains much imaginary conversation. The Bartholomew volume traces the fantastic story behind the chain of killings beginning with Charles Webb and ending with Elijah Briant: Charles Webb killed by Wes Hardin; Hardin killed by John Selman; Selman killed by George Scarborough; Scarborough killed by Will Carver; and Carver killed by Elijah Briant. A thorough researcher, Ed Bartholomew has brought to light considerable information on and authentic photographs of the gunmen and badmen of the old West.

The latest biography, *John Wesley Hardin, Texas Gunman* (New York, 1957), by Lewis Nordyke, is the best yet written on Hardin. Nordyke included a great deal of new information in his carefully prepared account. He was allowed access to the letters and documents in the possession of the Hardin descendants and in the family of Fred Duderstadt, Hardin's good friend who helped rear his children. Hardin's own story was used only as a guide from which to check original sources. In a letter to me, Mr. Nordyke stated that he was able to document every major incident in the life of Hardin. Some of Hardin's accounts are slanted according to his personal views, as is to be expected; nevertheless, Wes's story is much more accurate than the accounts contemporary historians and biographers have written about him.

A recent book, *Frontier Newspaper: The El Paso* Times (El Paso, 1958), by John Middagh, gives an excellent account of Hardin's final days as reported in the columns of the El Paso *Times* in 1895.

The first copies of *The Life of John Wesley Hardin, as Written by Himself* contained a portrait labeled "John Wesley Hardin." Ramon F. Adams, in his excellent bibliography, claims that this is a portrait of Joe Hardin, brother of Wes. Apparently someone called the publisher's hand on this photograph, for after a few copies were released, there was substituted a photograph of a young fellow with a mustache and curly hair, which also was listed as being an authentic photograph of John Wesley Hardin. It, however, bears little or no resemblance to the authentic pictures of John Wesley Hardin. Ramon Adams believes it is one the printers had on hand and has no relation whatever to any member of the Hardin family. The book also contains a cut of Manning Clements, a relative of Hardin's, which compares favorably to known photographs of Clements. Four pen-and-ink sketches depicting dramatic episodes in the career of Hardin also appear in the book. These were drawn by J. Onderdonk.

This reprint of *The Life of John Wesley Hardin* in the Western Frontier Library is the second such release. A paperback reprint was brought out in a small edition by J. Marvin Hunter and his *Frontier Times* magazine in 1926.

The following book is an accurate and amazing account of one of the West's most notorious badmen and gunslingers. As practically the only source of information about John Wesley Hardin, it is indeed a worthy addition to the Western Frontier Library.

I would like to thank those who gave generous assistance in the preparation of this introduction. My good friend Carl W. Breihan, the author of several fine books on Western outlaws, gave freely of his knowledge and advice. Lewis Nordyke responded immediately to my request for information uncovered by him in preparing his excellent biography of Hardin. My thanks also to R. N. Mullin for his aid and encouragement. Ramon Adams, Loring Campbell, and Ed Bartholomew helped with their vast knowledge of the outlaws of the West and the books about them. And I would like to thank also William F. Kelleher, that eminent dealer in Western books of Cliffside Park, N. J.

Pasadena, Texas   ROBERT G. MCCUBBIN

THE LIFE OF
JOHN WESLEY HARDIN

PREFACE

IN PRESENTING THIS AUTOBIOGRAPHY of John Wesley Hardin to the public, we feel sure that to many a new light will thus be thrown on the life and character of the most notorious desperado Texas ever produced. The deeds that men do live after them, and to the new generation the name of John Wesley Hardin is associated with the most desperate crimes and blood-thirsty atrocities ever printed in a 5-cent novel. By reading these pages a certain justice will be done his memory. Hardin, in the latter years of his life, often reiterated that he had never killed a man wantonly or in cold blood, and we believe that this book, evidently written without any purpose of self-justification, will bear him out. The manuscript itself is written in a clear, blunt, and direct style, and is given to the public with little, if any, alteration. Hardin was a born leader of men, whether for good or evil, and had it not been for the unfortunate surroundings of his boyhood days, would undoubtedly have made a mark in civil life. His determination, often amounting to the most daring and unreasonable obstinacy, may be traced through this self-told story of his life and can be even detected in the bold lines of his handwriting. Brave, reckless, and daring he certainly was, and he loved his wife and children with depth and tenderness. He was a daring character in daring times, born with an utter contempt

3

for the consequences of yielding to a high and fierce temper. Such, in brief, is the framework of the life of the intrepid character to be found in these pages. To the Hon. P. S. Sowell, member of the Legislature from Guadalupe County, we are indebted for being enabled to publish this manuscript. With marked legal ability he fought for the claim of the Hardin children through the El Paso courts, finally securing this manuscript for the heirs.

The short appendix to be found at the conclusion is compiled from letters and papers found among his effects and is published with the consent of his children.

THE LIFE OF
John Wesley Hardin

——

I WAS BORN in Bonham, Fannin County, Texas, on the 26th of May, 1853. My father, J. G. Hardin, was a Methodist preacher and circuit rider. My mother, Elizabeth Hardin, was a blonde, highly cultured, and charity predominated in her disposition. She made my father a model wife and helpmate. My father continued to travel his circuit as a preacher until 1869, when he moved and located near Moscow, in Polk County, on account of bad health. In the same year he moved again, this time to Sumpter, in Trinity County, where he taught school. He organized and established an academy, to which institution he sent my elder brother, Joe G. Hardin, and myself. In the meantime my father was studying law, and in 1861 was admitted to the bar. The War between the States had broken out at this time and while my father had voted against secession, yet, when his State seceded, he went with his State and immediately organized a company to fight and, if need be, to die for Southern rights. He was elected captain of this company, but resigned at the solicitation of the best citizens, Capt. Ballinger being elected to the command. So my father stayed at home because, as said the foremost men of the community, "You can be of more good use at home than off fighting Yankees." Although I was but 9 years old at this time, I had already conceived the idea of running off and going with a cousin to fight Yankees. But my father got on to the little game and put an end to it all by giving me a sound thrashing. Still the principles of the Southern cause loomed up in my mind ever bigger, brighter, and stronger as the months and years rolled on. I had seen Abraham Lincoln burned and shot to pieces in effigy so often that I looked upon him as a very demon incarnate, who was waging a relentless and cruel war on the South to rob her of her most sacred rights. So you can see that the justice of the Southern cause was taught to me in my youth, and if I never relinquished these teachings in after years, surely I was but true to my early training. The way you bend a twig, that is the way it will grow, is an old saying, and a true one. So I grew up a rebel. In 1862 my father moved to Livingston, in Polk County, where he taught school and practiced law. In 1865 we again moved back to Sumpter, my father still teaching and practicing law, my brother and I being regular scholars. Our parents had taught us from our infancy to be honest, truthful, and brave, and we were taught that no brave boy would let another call him a liar with impunity, consequently we had lots of battles with other boys at school. I was naturally active and strong and always came out best, though sometimes with a bleeding nose, scratched face, or a black eye; but true to my early training, I would try, try, try again. We continued in Sumpter at school for some time, and of course I received the biggest part of my education there. I always tried to excel in my studies, and generally stood at the head. Being playful by nature, I was generally first on the playground at recess and noon. Marbles, rolly hole, cat, bull pen, and town ball were our principal games, and I was considered by my schoolmates an expert. I knew how to knock the middle man, throw a hot ball, and ply the bat. Of course, we had examinations and school exhibitions, which were creditable to all concerned, but in 1867 an incident occurred which I think proper to relate. We were preparing for an examination when one of my schoolmates and myself had an almost fatal fight. His name was Charles Sloter, and as he wanted to be the boss among the boys, of course I stood in his way. In order to "down" me, he publicly accused me of writing some doggerel on the wall about one "Sal," a girl scholar. It commenced, "I love Sal, and Sal loves mutton," and ended in some reflections upon Sal's personal attractions. I knew that he was the author of the poetry, and when he accused me of writing it, I at once denied it and proved it up on him. He came over to my seat in the school room, struck me and drew his knife. I stabbed him twice almost fatally in the breast and back. A howl at once went up to expel me from the school, some even wanting to hang me. The trustees, however, heard the true facts in the case and instead of expelling me, completely exonerated me and the courts acquitted me.

I may mention here that poor Charley was long afterwards hung by a mob in an adjoining county.

Now, as I am about to leave the story of my boyish days and enter upon the description of a course of life which, when once entered on, few live to reach their majority, I deem it proper to say a few words more about the way my early days were spent before going on further with the history of my life. I was always a very child of nature, and her ways and moods were my study. My greatest pleasure was to be out in the open fields, the forests, and the swamps. My greatest pleasure was to get out among the big pines and oaks with my gun and the dogs and kill deer, coons, 'possums, or wild cats. If any of those Sumpter boys with whom I used to hunt ever see this history of my life, I ask them to say whether or not our sport in those old days was not splendid. John Norton, Bill Gordon, Shiles and Hiram Frazier, and Sol Adams, all of Sumpter, can all bear witness to the good times we had then.

We were still living in Polk County when my father took up the idea that he would improve his headright, situated about three miles northwest of Livingstone, bordering on Long King Creek. Capt. T. L. Eperson of Livingstone conceived the same idea about his headright at the same time as my father, and I believe he made a success of his venture in farming. Not so my father. He soon became disgusted with country life and actually gave his headright farm and improvements on it to his brother, Barnett Hardin, and wife, whose name was Anne. I do not know the reason of this generosity, but believe it was in order that neither he, his wife, nor his children should ever be bothered with the plague of ticks that infested the place. Of all the places I have ever been I believe that to have been the most accursedly "ticky." I believe now my father to have been a most wise man in giving that place away. When we were improving it, we had six or eight colored men clearing up, rail splitting, building houses, etc. It is needless to say that my brother Joe and myself spent most of our time out there with the Negroes, dogs, and, of course, the ticks. What a big time we had hunting and fishing with them! (The ticks, as well as the Negroes and dogs, for the ticks went wherever we did.) I remember a hunt I got into by my lone self which is worth narrating before I leave my early days. We had a horse named Jack, which had strayed away, and we finally heard of him at old Mr. Sikes', about three miles and a half west of our place. I was told to go and get Jack, so next morning, after locating his whereabouts, I called my dogs, got my bridle and a rope, and started out afoot after

Jack. I got to old Bob Sikes' place, found Jack there, and of course the old man would have me stay to dinner. I ate heartily as the meal was gotten up in good country style. It was late when I started back to the Hardin camp with Jack and my dogs. It was drizzling rain and the skies looked black. We had about three and a half miles of dense wood to go through, and report had it that wild animals abounded there. However, I had great confidence in Jack and my dogs, and nothing but a ghost could scare me unless it was lightning. I started the dogs out, and presently I heard old Watch bark and later on I heard the others all baying as if they had sure enough found something. I took the course and, after going a mile, found Watch at the foot of a big white-oak tree, looking up and gnawing at the base, while the other dogs were about twenty yards off looking up into the branches of the big oak. I looked up and finally made out four big coons up at the very top of the tree. Now I wanted those coons to take to camp as a trophy of my trip. I knew that Joe would laud me to the skies if I succeeded in getting them, and it meant a big stew for all hands that night. There were no limbs for me to reach, so I decided to ride Jack up close to the trunk, stand up on his back, and throw the rope over the lowest limb. I did this, trusting to Jack to stand still and not run off. The next two limbs were away above me, but with the use of the rope I got to the limb where the coons were. The coons, however, concluding the situation was getting decidedly hot, decided to charge me. They began to form in line, one behind the other, to growl and show fight. Meanwhile I had tied myself securely to the tree and had broken off a bough to defend myself with. Here came the coons and attacked me at once. I struck right and left with my weapon, but it broke in pieces the first lick, so I had nothing left but my

9

fists. I fought hard and long, and one by one I knocked those coons out of that tree top fifty feet high, and they no sooner hit the ground than the dogs made short work of them. I then untied myself from the tree, and with the use of the rope reached the ground a wiser, if not a braver, boy. I was covered with blood from head to foot; my hands, face, and breast were torn and lacerated, being badly bitten and scratched. I had to leave my rope up on the first limb, so when I dropped to the ground, I piled the coons up and tied them together with my galluses. I then sat down and made a rope out of my breeches to lead the faithful Jack. I was in a nice fix now; three miles from home, raining, a loose horse, four coons, and three dogs, going through a swamp in my shirt tail and night coming on. To make matters worse, Jack rebelled against packing those coons. Of all the pitching, jumping, and kicking you ever saw, Jack did it then. After considerable begging and coaxing I finally induced Jack to let me and the coons ride. We all struck out for camp and got there after dark. On our arrival we had a regular jollification. They told me that they wondered why I was not lying a dead boy in that swamp after such an experience. I told them that it was pluck that both saved me and captured the coons. Here I wish to tell my readers that if there is any power to save a man, woman, or child from harm, outside the power of the Living God, it is this thing called pluck. I never was afraid of anything except ghosts, and I have lived that down now and they have no terrors for me. Constant association with Negroes in my young days had made me superstitious in this respect, and I was well versed in old folklore about ghosts, spirits, dead men's shadows, graveyards, etc., and many a time then did I honestly believe I had seen them.

The first man I ever saw killed I will now tell you about.

His name was Turner Evans and he was killed by old John Ruff in the town of Sumpter, Trinity County, Texas, in the year 1861. My father had just organized his company of soldiers to go to the seat of war at Richmond. I remember the day well. Ruff was a poor man and owed Turner Evans. Evans was overbearing and, besides running an attachment on Ruff's property, annoyed him greatly in every way. Late in the evening Evans began to drink, and being rich and influential, had a crowd of hangers on around him. Fired by whisky he began late in the evening to go around town from store to store inquiring for Ruff, declaring that he would cane him wherever he found him. At last he found him in a small grocery store and at once commenced to curse and abuse him. Ruff said: "Turner, you have ruined me financially and now come with your crowd to attack me personally. Go off." Evans said: "I will, after I have caned you," and so saying he struck him over the head with his cane. Ruff pulled a large Bowie knife and started for Evans. Evans' friends hit Ruff with chairs and tried to stop him, while Evans himself used his stick freely. Ruff, however, was by this time a determined and angry man, and cut at everybody that tried to stop him. He finally cut Evans down, and the sheriff appearing on the scene, Ruff was at once arrested. Evans' friends carried him off, but his wounds were fatal, the jugular vein being completely severed, and he soon died and left a large family. Ruff, after lying in jail for several years, came clear. Readers, you see what drink and passion will do. If you wish to be successful in life, be temperate and control your passions; if you don't, ruin and death is the inevitable result.

In the fall of 1868, I went down to my uncle's (Barnett Hardin) in Polk County, about four miles north of Livingstone. I was in the habit of making these trips, though I was then but 15 years old. This time they were making sugar and I took the trip to see them, carrying my pistol of course. I met a Negro named Mage close to Moscow who had belonged to Judge Houlshousen, a brother to my Uncle Barnett Hardin's wife. I had a cousin named Barnett Jones who matched himself and me against this Moscow Negro in a wrestling bout. The Negro was a large, powerful man, and we were but two boys. Nevertheless we threw him down the first fall. He was not satisfied, so we threw him again, and this time scratched his face a little and made it bleed. Negro like, he got mad and said he could whip me and would do it. Barnett and others standing around stopped us from fighting. This seemed to make Mage all the more angry. He said he would kill me, and went after his gun. I went up to the house to get mine, too, but Uncle Barnett got on to the game and made me stay in the house, while that Negro went around cursing and abusing me, saying "that he would kill me or die himself; that no white boy could draw his blood and live; that a bird never flew too high not to come to the ground." Uncle Barnett then took a hand and ordered Mage off the plantation. The next morning I had to start home and go about seven or eight miles out of the way to deliver a message from my father to old Capt. Sam Rowes. About six miles from Capt. Rowes' place and eight from Judge Houlshousen's, I overtook the Negro Mage. He was walking and had a stout stick in his hand. A small creek ran to the east of the road, which made a sharp bend of about 100 yards, and from bend to bend ran a path. Just as I overtook Mage he took the path while a stayed in the main road. He had gone about fifteen steps before he turned and saw me. He recognized me at once and began to curse and abuse me, saying that I was a coward for not shooting it out last night. I told him that I was

12

but playing with him when I scratched him and did not intend to hurt him. He answered by saying that if he could but get hold of me he would kill me and throw me in the creek; that he believed he could outrun old Paint (the horse I was riding, and a very poor one) and catch me anyway. I told him to go his way and let me go mine, and whipped old Paint into a trot. Mage, seeing this, ran along the path to where it again met the main road and cut me off. He cursed me again and threatened me with death.

I stopped in the road and he came at me with his big stick. He struck me, and as he did it I pulled out a Colt's .44 six-shooter and told him to get back. By this time he had my horse by the bridle, but I shot him loose. He kept coming back, and every time he would start I would shoot again and again until I shot him down. I went to Uncle Clabe Houlshousen and brought him and another man back to where Mage was lying. Mage still showed fight and called me a liar. If it had not been for my uncle, I would have shot him again. Uncle Houlshousen gave me a $20 gold piece and told me to go home and tell father all about the big fight; that Mage was bound to die, and for me to look out for the Yankee soldiers who were all over the country at that time. Texas like other states, was then overrun with carpet-baggers and bureau agents who had the United States Army to back them up in their meanness. Mage shortly died in November, 1868. This was the first man I ever killed, and it nearly distracted my father and mother when I told them. All the courts were then conducted by bureau agents and renegades, who were the inveterate enemies of the South and administered a code of justice to suit every case that came before them and which invariably ended in gross injustice to Southern people, especially to those who still openly held on to the principles of the

South. To be tried at that time for the killing of a Negro meant certain death at the hands of a court, backed by Northern bayonets; hence my father told me to keep in hiding until that good time when the Yankee bayonet should cease to govern. Thus, unwillingly, I became a fugitive, not from justice be it known, but from the injustice and misrule of the people who had subjugated the South. I had an elder brother teaching school on Logallis Prairie, about twenty-five miles north of Sumpter, so I went up there intending in a few weeks to go to Navarro County, where I had relatives. So I stayed at old man Morgan's in an out-of-the-way place and spent my time hunting wild cattle and game. In a little while the United States soldiers heard of my whereabouts and came after me. My brother, however, had heard of their coming and had told me. I soon was after them instead of they after me. We met in the bed of a deep creek and after a sharp fight two white soldiers lay dead, while a Negro soldier was flying for his life. I ran up on him and demanded his surrender in the name of the Southern Confederacy. He answered me with a shot, when I brought him to the ground with a bullet from my Colt's .44. All this was kept very secret, and these soldiers were buried in the bed of the creek about 100 yards below where the fight took place. I knew they would cross the creek where they did so. I waylaid them, as I had no mercy on men whom I knew only wanted to get my body to torture and kill. It was war to the knife with me, and I brought it on by opening the fight with a double-barreled shotgun and ending it with a cap-and-ball six-shooter. Thus it was that by the fall of 1868 I had killed four men and was myself wounded in the arm. Parties in the neighborhood of the last fight took the soldiers' horses, and as we burned all their effects, everything was kept quiet.

In January, 1869, I went with my father to Navarro County and engaged in school teaching near Pisga. I had about twenty-five scholars, both girls and boys, from the age of 6 to 16 years. I taught school for three months at the old Word schoolhouse, and when the term was out the school was offered to me again. I had, however, conceived the idea of becoming a cowboy, and as my cousins were in the business, I began to drive cattle to shipping points. Of course, in this kind of a life I soon learned how to play poker, seven-up, and euchre, and it was but a short time until I would banter the best for a game. I liked fast horses and soon would bet on any kind of a horse race, a chicken fight, a dog fight, or anything down to throwing "crack-a-loo," or spitting at a mark.

In those times if there was anything that could rouse my passion it was seeing impudent Negroes lately freed insult or abuse old, wounded Confederates who were decrepit, weak, or old. There were lots of those kind in the country in the sixties, and these Negroes bullied both them and even the weaker sex whenever they had the advantage. Frequently I involved myself in almost inextricable difficulties in this way. Once I learned that in one of the eastern counties there was a most insulting and bulldozing Negro bully who made it a point to insult these decrepit old men, and who paid no respect to white ladies. In short, he was a terror to the community. I thought over this until I determined to see what could be done to stop him and his wickedness. I went to that neighborhood and found out when he was in the habit of going to town. I dressed myself as an old man and met him in the road. Of course, when we met I would not give him the road, and he at once commenced his tirade of abuse. I told him that I was old and feeble and lived in a distant country, but that I was a

Southerner and did not want a big burly Negro to treat me the way he was doing. This enraged him. He stopped his steers, jumped down off his wagon, and commenced to pop his whip at me, calling me vile names and low-down white trash. He popped me at last and I could not stand it any longer. I pulled off my mask, drew my six-shooter and told him to say his prayers. I told him I was going to kill him for his cruelty to white folks, but did not want to send him before his Maker without a chance to repent. He certainly prayed a prayer. "Jesus have mercy on dis bad nigger, and have mercy on all de poor white men and keep dis young white man from killing dis bad nigger." About this time my pistol went off and his prayer abruptly ended. The ball did not strike the Negro, but it had the desired effect, for it reformed him completely. That Negro afterwards became one of the best citizens of that county; became civil and polite and was never known to insult a white person, male or female, after that.

While living near Pisga, in Navarro County, I had made the acquaintance of nearly everybody there at that time. I knew the notorious desperado Frank Polk, who was finally killed at Wortham in Limestone County while resisting arrest after having killed the mayor of that town.

I knew the Newmans, the Tramels, the Rushings; the Andersons and Dixons were cousins of mine. I may mention here that I met Jim Newman quite lately, and in talking over old times near Pisga in 1869, he asked me if I remembered how some fellow jumped when I shot at him. I told him, "Yes, I remember it." "Well," said Jim Newman, "I bet you at that time that you could not shoot his eye out, and we had a bottle of whisky on it; come in, now; it is my treat." I suppose I won the bet but did not recollect

16

it after so many years. This same Jim Newman is now sheriff of Nolan County; his post office is Sweetwater.

Frank Polk had killed a man named Tom Brady, and a detachment of Yankees came out from Corsicana to capture Polk and myself. They, as usual, failed on me, but got Frank. They carried him to Corsicana, where, after a long confinement, he finally came clear. At that time I had a cousin named Simp Dixon, who belonged to the "Ku Kluck Klan" and was sworn to kill Yankee soldiers as long as he lived. He had been raised in northern Texas, but was forced to fly from there. His mother, brother, and sister were tortured and killed by the United States soldiers because of their loyalty to the Southern cause. Simp, therefore, had good cause for hating the Yankees. There was a big reward for Simp, and so, of course, I sympathized with him in every way and was generally with him. On one occasion in the Richland bottom a squad of soldiers ran up on us and a pitched battle immediately ensued. It was a free and fast fight. When the battle was over, two soldiers lay dead. Simp killed one and I killed the other, while the rest escaped. Simp was afterwards killed by a squad of United States soldiers at Cotton Gin, in Limestone County. He was undoubtedly one of the most dangerous men in Texas. He was born in Fannin County in 1850 and was about 19 years old at the time of his death.

Late in the fall of 1869 my brother, Joe Hardin, came to see me and persuaded me to leave Navarro County, which I consented to do, and we went into Hill County, stopping a short time at Hillsboro with Aunt Anne Hardin and family and then going out some seven or eight miles into the county to Uncle Barnett Hardin's. We then went down the Brazos to some relatives of ours named Page, where I speculated in cotton and hides. I played poker and seven-up whenever I got a chance and once in a while would bet on a pony race. These races generally came off on the old Boles track near Towash. A man named John Collins had married a cousin of mine, and I went into partnership with him. Things ran smoothly for some time and we were doing well until a tragedy occurred that forever dissolved our partnership. I had been receiving letters from my father and mother urging me to quit my wild habits and turn to better ways. They wrote that they were going to move down to the Page settlement so that they could be with me. On the 24th of December my father came to see me and brought me good news from all the loved ones at home, and telling me that they had all moved to Navarro County. Next day was Christmas day and I borrowed my father's horse, a pretty good runner, to go to the grocery and the races at the old Boles track. Collins and I had matched some races to be run on that day, but of course we never told my father about this. There were a lot of Arkansas people there with horses; especially do I remember Hamp Davis and Jim Bradly. We came very near having a shooting match several times that day, as everybody in the '60's carried pistols, but all left the track apparently satisfied. Jim Bradly, whom I have mentioned above, was introduced to me as a desperado and a killer. I have been reliably informed that he was there for my especial benefit, but in those days an unknown desperado had as much influence on me as a snaffle bit on a wild horse. After the races about fifteen or twenty of us went to a grocery near by kept by Dire & Jenkins; there was a gin there and one or two stores. We soon got into a poker game. I had won $50 or $75 on the races and had $325 besides, thus having about $400 in all. At this time I was but 16 years old. It was arranged that Collins,

18

my·partner, was not to play, but Jim Bradly (the Arkansas bully) had borrowed his six-shooter. The game was composed of Jim Bradly, Hamp Davis, Judge Moore, and myself. I knew afterwards that these three stood in against me, but did not know this at the time. One thing, however, I did know, and that was how to protect myself pretty well from such fellows in a game of draw poker. I placed about $350 in gold in front of me and about $10 in silver. Bradly, on my left, placed in front of himself about $5 in silver and $20 in gold; Davis, on Bradly's left, about $10 in silver and $40 in gold, and Moore about $30 in gold. The game proceeded quietly until about 12 o'clock at night, about which time I had won all the money. We were playing on a blanket in a small box house without a door but with a place open for a chimney in the north end. The house was about 13x14 feet and was situated about a quarter of a mile from the grocery. The moon was shining brightly and the night was clear and cold. I had won all the money on the blanket, as I said before, and all the players owed me. I had pulled off my boots and thrown them in the corner to my left next to Bradly, not suspecting that robbery was the intention of the game. I was quietly fixing to quit the game unknown to the others and had put all the gold in my pocket, only having about $25 or $30 in front of me. Moore remarked that everybody owed Hardin. I said, "Yes," but Jim Bradly said no, and we left it to Moore and Davis to decide. They said, "Yes, you owe Hardin $5." About this time we both got good hands and I bet him $5 on three aces. He made me put up the money but "called" me without putting up a cent. I said to him: "Now you owe me $10, let us settle up or quit." He said: "You are a g—— d—— liar and a coward," drew a big knife, and quick as a cat could wink made a grab for me, while Davis got my

19

six-shooter in the corner. Collins then threw himself between Bradly and me and kept him from stabbing me to
death. This gave me a chance to get up, and when I did
Bradly drew his six-shooter and threatened to kill me if I
did not give up my money. "Give me $500 or I will kill
you, g—— d—— you," he said. Collins came to my rescue
again and grabbed him, crying to me to jump out of the
chimney opening or I would be killed. Out I went, barefooted on the frosty ground, and ran out to our horses.
Davis gave me a fearful cursing, calling me a murderer, a
coward, a robber, and saying he would get me before day.
Collins came out to where I was standing behind a tree and
said: "John, let us go home; we are in a hell of a scrape."
I said: "Where is your pistol?" He said: "Bradly borrowed
it in the early part of the night." "No," I said, "I am not
going home to face my father in this condition; I want my
boots, my money, and my pistol. Don't be a fool, but take
things coolly." Collins went back to get my boots, which
Bradly finally gave him permission to do. Bradly continued
to abuse me and went to the grocery with his crowd, who
by this time were all cursing me as a man who had been
posing as a brave man, but who in fact was a coward and
a damned rascal. As soon as I got my boots on, I told
Collins I wanted to go and see Moore, who had my money
and pistol. He said he would go with me to his boarding
house, as he knew the proprietor. We left our horses where
they were and found Moore at the boarding house. He refused to give up either the pistol or the money without
Bradly's consent. He agreed to go with Collins to see Bradly
at the grocery about 100 yards off across the road in an
easterly direction. When they got to the grocery and saw
Bradly, he was still cursing. He threatened Collins and swore
he would kill me if he saw me. Moore told him I was at

his boarding house after my pistol and money. Bradly said, "Well, I'll go over there and fill him full of lead." Meantime Collins had borrowed a pistol and persuaded Bradly to exchange, telling him he was going home and wanted his own. John Collins bade him good-bye and came back to the boarding house where I was. He wanted me to go home, but by this time Bradly had started over to where I was, swearing to kill me. The proprietor was trying to get me to leave, when I asked him for a pistol to defend myself with from robbery and death. He refused to do this, but Collins gave me his and said, "Now let us go to our horses." I said, "All O.K.," and we started to go out of the gate and into the public road that led to where our horses were. Just as we got out of the gate we saw Bradly with six or seven others, including Hamp Davis, coming toward us, threatening to kill me, his crowd urging him on by shouting, "Go for him! We are with you," etc. I told John Collins to go in the lead. The gin was on the right, about fifty yards away, with a store about fifty yards from where we were standing. Bradly saw me and tried to cut me off, getting in front of me with a pistol in one hand and a Bowie knife in the other. He commenced to fire on me, firing once, then snapping, and then firing again. By this time we were within five or six feet of each other, and I fired with a Remington .45 at his heart and right after that at his head. As he staggered and fell, he said, "O, Lordy, don't shoot me any more." I could not stop. I was shooting because I did not want to take chances on a reaction. The crowd ran, and I stood there and cursed them loud and long as cowardly devils who had urged a man to fight and when he did and fell, to desert him like cowards and traitors. I went to my horse, rode over to Frank Shelton's, borrowed a gun, came back, and demanded my money, but received no answer. I went on to where my father was at old Jim Page's and got there at 2 A.M. I woke him up and told him what had happened. It was a great blow to him, for he had been counting on taking me back home with him. I told him I would go home anyway, but would keep on the west side of the Brazos River until the next night. I soon found out the situation was critical. The whole country, with the exception of a few friends and relatives, had turned out to hunt me; in fact, there was a regular mob after me, whose avowed purpose was to hang me. I had agreed with my father to meet him at a certain place on the night of the 26th, but they watched him so closely that he could not come. He had a trusted Masonic friend, however, named Martin, whom he sent to post me as to what was going on. Directly after Martin had left me, a posse of some fifteen men ran up and surrounded me in a cotton pen. I told them that if they were officers to send one or two men and I would surrender, but I would not yield to a mob. They answered that I must give up or take the consequences. I replied, "Consequences be damned. Light in if you think there is no bottom." I commenced to pump lead at them and they cried, "Hold up." They then sent two men up to demand my surrender. When they came, I covered them with a double-barreled shotgun and told them their lives depended on their actions, and unless they obeyed my orders to the letter, I would shoot first one and then the other. They readily assented. "Tell your friends out there," I said, "that Hardin has surrendered and that they had better go home or meet you at old Jim Page's, that Hardin is afraid of a mob." They did so and the crowd moved off toward Page's. When they were out of sight, I made both men with me lay down their arms. One had a double-barreled gun and two six-shooters; the other had a rifle and two der-

22

ringers. They complied with my request under the potent persuasion of my gun levelled first on one and then the other. I then got on my horse and told those fellows to follow their pals to Jim Page's; that I would be along directly and to wait for me there. I reckon they are waiting for me there yet. I went off to the west, but soon changed to the east; went through Hillsboro and into Navarro County. There I saw my dear mother and my brothers and sisters. Soon after, my father came and brought me the news that they were hot after me and were going to Pisga hoping to find me there. I got together three or four of my best friends and went to meet them. We met them on the west side of the Pinoak, about six miles from Pisga. They denied they were after me. I told them to go back to Jim Page's where I was going and where an arresting party was now waiting for me. I told them if they had a legal warrant to show it and I would give up. They said they had none. Thereupon one of my party took occasion to tell them they had gone far enough towards Pisga and that if they loved their wives and children to go back to Hillsboro. They went. I went back to Pisga, fixed up my affairs with Aleck Barrickman, and started for Brenham on the 20th of January, 1870. I intended to visit my uncle, Bob Hardin, there. About 25 miles from Pisga a circus was going on at a place called Horn Hill. One of the circus men had had a row with some of the citizens, resulting in some men being shot. We knew nothing about this and upon getting to town went to an hotel to get a bed. The circus people had all the beds engaged, so we could not get a one. About 10 P.M. we went out to the circus campfires. It was quite cold and while we were all standing round the fire I accidentally struck the hand of a circus man who was lighting his pipe with a fagot from the fire. I begged his pardon at once and assured him it was a pure accident. He, however, just roared and bellowed and swore he would "smash my nose." I told him to smash and be damned, that I was a kind of a smasher myself. He said: "You are, are you?" struck me on the nose, and started to pull his gun. I pulled mine and fired. He fell with a .45 ball through his head. Barrickman covered the crowd until we could make a truce. I saddled our horses and we rode off, apparently to the north, but soon changed our course south. We met nobody who knew us, so after Barrickman had ridden with me about sixteen miles, he returned to Pisga and I went on to Brenham by way of Kosse, Calvert, and Bryant. I was young then and loved every pretty girl I met, and at Kosse I met one and we got along famously together. I made an engagement to call on her that night and did so. I had not been there long when someone made a row at the door of the house. She got scared and told me it was her sweetheart, and about this time the fellow came in and told me he would kill me if I did not give him $100. I told him to go slow, and not to be in such a hurry; that I only had about $50 or $60 in my pocket, but if he would go with me to the stable I would give him more as I had the money in my saddle pockets. He said he would go, and I, pretending to be scared, started for the stable. He said, "Give me what you have got first." I told him all right, and in so doing, dropped some of it on the floor. He stooped down to pick it up and as he was straightening up I pulled my pistol and fired. The ball struck him between the eyes and he fell over, a dead robber. I stopped long enough to get back most of my money and resumed my journey to Brenham. I arrived there about the last of January, 1870, and went to Uncle Bob Hardin's, who was then improving his place. He persuaded me to farm with him and his boys, William, Aaron, and

24

Joe. All the money I had I gave to my aunt to keep for me. I thus became a farmer and made a good plough boy and hoer. I would often want to go to Brenham and did go with William or Aaron or Joe. I used to find it hard to get my money from my good aunt. I used to tell her I had to go to town to get me a pair of shoes or a hat and that she could not suit me if she went. On one occasion I won about $60 at roulette, and when I brought my aunt the money, she wanted to know where I got that money. I told her with a laugh that I had that money all the time. On another occasion Will and I rode our best horses to town and hitched them to the courthouse fence. When we got through "sporting" and came back for our horses, we found them gone. They had evidently been stolen, and though we rode a hundred miles or more, we never laid eyes on those horses again.

I met a good many well-known characters on those trips to Brenham. I used to gamble a good deal and it was there I got the name of "Young Seven-up." I met Phil Coe first there in Brenham, that notorious Phil Coe who was afterwards killed in Abilene, Kansas, by "Wild Bill." I stayed at my uncle's until the crops were laid by, and though prospects were splendid, the country was getting pretty hot for me. The State Police had been organized and McAnally had been placed on the force, so on consultation with friends, it was thought best that I should leave Brenham. I sold out my interest in the crop and again started on my roaming life. I first went to Evergreen, about 40 miles from Brenham. There were some races there and the town was full of hard characters. Bill Longley and Ben Hinds were there, as was also Jim Brown. In those days they gambled in the open air out in the streets when the weather permitted. Ben Hinds and I commenced playing "seven-up" on a goods box, and I won about $20 from him, when I concluded to quit. He got mad and said if I was not a boy he would beat me to death. Ben was considered one of the most dangerous men in the country, but in those days I made no distinction in men as fighters. I told him I stood in men's shoes and not to spoil a good intention on account of my youth. He yelled at me: "You damned little impudent scoundrel, I'll beat hell out of you." As he made for me, I covered him with my pistol and told him I was a little on the scrap myself, the only difference between him and I being that I used lead. About this time a dozen men had gathered around. Some of them tried to catch me and others started to draw their pistols. I said, "The first man that makes a move or draws a gun I'll kill him." At the same time I drew my other pistol and made them all get in front of me, saying that I wanted no back action in this fight. You bet they got in front of me in short order. Ben then said, "Young man, I was wrong, I beg your pardon. You are a giant with a youth's face. Even if you are a boy I bow to you, and here is my hand in good faith." I answered, "I can not take your hand, but I accept your apology in good faith." Ben said, "I will be your friend; don't be uneasy while you are here; Bill Longley will be at the races tomorrow, so stop over and we will have a good time."

Late that evening a dark-looking man came to me and said, "My name is Bill Longley and I believe you are a spy for McAnally. If you don't watch out, you will be shot all to pieces before you know it."

I said, "You believe a damned lie, and all I ask is that those who are going to do the shooting will get in front of me. All I ask is a fair fight, and if your name is Bill Longley I want you to understand that you can't bulldoze or scare me."

26

Bill replied, "I see I have made a mistake. Are you here to see the races?"

I told him "not particularly." He invited me to stay over and see the horses. We went and struck a poker game going on in a crib. We both got into the game. Directly it came my turn to deal. I had three jacks to go on and raised $5. All stayed in, and in the draw Bill drew three cards, while the other two players drew one apiece. I drew two and caught the other jack. Bill filled on aces. One of the other players made a flush, and the other filled on queens. The flush man bet $5, the man with a full went $10 better. I studied a while and said, "You can't run me out on my own deal, so I go $10 better." Bill Longley said, "Well, stranger, you have your foot in it now; I go you $50 better." The man with a flush passed; the man with a queen full says, "Bill, I call a sight."

Bill says, "All right; how much money have you got?"

He counted out $45.

"Well, stranger," said Bill, "it's up to you. What do you do?"

I said, "What are you betting 'wind or money?' "

He said, "Money."

"Put it up," said I.

He went down in his pocket and pulled out four $20 gold pieces and took out a $5 gold piece.

I said, "All right, here is your $50 and I go you $250 better."

He said, "I go you; I call you."

I told him to put up the money. He asked me if his word was not good, and I told him no. He went into his pocket again and pulled out eleven $20 gold pieces and asked me if I would credit him for the balance. I told him no.

"Well," he said, "I call you for $220."

I told him all right. "I reckon you have me beat."

He said, "I reckon so. I have got an ace full."

I said, "Hold on, I have two pair."

He said, "They are not worth a damn."

I said, "I reckon two pair of jacks are good," so the eventful game ended. I was ahead about $300.

Some way or another they all got on to my identity, and they all treated me with a good deal of respect at the races the next day.

I went west and stopped at Round Rock in Williamson County to see my old schoolmaster, J. C. Landrum. I had been his pupil in the '60's at Sumpter. After this I concluded to go north from there as I had relatives in Navarro and Limestone counties. I naturally wanted to see them, even if I had to take risks in doing so. I still cherished the hope that the day would come when I could stand my trial and come clear. My father always told me that when the Democrats regained power, I could get a fair trial, but I could never expect that under carpet-bag rule. Of course I had long ago concluded not to surrender for the present, and whenever force was unlawfully employed to make me do so, I met it with force, or else got out of the way.

In August, 1870, I went to Navarro and stayed at Pisga, where I gambled a while. From there I went to Mount Calm, where my father was teaching school. There I peddled in hides and traded, making some money.

Soon after, I got a letter from my brother Joe, who was going to school at Round Rock to Professor Landrum. I also got one from the professor himself, both letters urging me to come up there and graduate with Joe. I went up there but only went to school for one day. The rewards that were offered for me made that country too dangerous a place for me to stop. I passed my diploma examination, however,

28

satisfactorily, so Joe and I graduated together. My brother Joe then went to Mount Calm, helped my father to teach school, and became a lawyer. He afterwards moved out to Comanche in 1872 and there lived until he met his death at the hands of a howling midnight mob of assassins in June, 1874. I concluded to go to Shreveport, La., where I had some relatives, and on my way there I stopped at a town named Longview. There they arrested me for another party, on a charge of which I was innocent. The State Police concluded to take me to Marshall, but I got out a writ of habeas corpus. I was, however, remanded to jail at Waco for some crime which I never committed. I was put in an old iron cell in the middle of the log jail, and nobody was allowed to see me. There were three other prisoners in there, and together we planned our escape. We were to wait until the food was brought in for supper and then we were to make our break. It was very cold weather when they first put me in jail, and I had money with me to buy whisky and tobacco for us all.

Thinking they would soon be released, they had offered to sell me a pistol, a .45 Colt with four barrels loaded. I unfolded my plan to them by which we could all get out. I was to cover the jailer as he opened the door and kill him if he did not obey orders. We were then all to rush out and stand the crowd off until dark would help us to easily get away.

They weakened, however, and so I bought the pistol for $10 in gold and a $25 overcoat. I had no idea when they were going to take me off, nor could I find out in any way. I tried to get them to go after my horse at Longview, but they would not do that.

One cold night they called for me, and I knew what was up, and you bet I was ready for them. I found out that I

29

was going because a Negro cook only brought up three supper plates. When the prisoners complained that there were only three plates and four of us, she said that "one of us was going to leave tonight." I prepared myself for an emergency. I had a very heavy fur coat, a medium sack coat, two undershirts, and two white shirts. I hid the pistol, tied with a good stout cord, under my left arm and over it my top shirt. I put on the rest of my clothes to see how it looked. It looked all right, so I took off my coat and vest and went to bed.

When they came to wake me up, I pretended to be awakened out of a sound sleep and to be very much surprised. They told me to get up and put on my clothes, that they were going to start for Waco with me. They told me I was wanted up there for killing Huffman in a barber shop. I appeared very much frightened and asked if there was any danger of a mob. Both Capt. Stokes and the jailer assured me that there was none. I then put on my vest and socks, putting a bottle of pickles in my overcoat pocket on the left side so as to make me look bulky. They searched me, but did not find any pistol. It was very cold and snow lay on the ground. They led up a little black pony with a blanket thrown over him for me to ride 225 miles to Waco. I asked where my own horse and saddle was, and they told me at Longview. I tried to buy a saddle from the jailer, but he would not sell me one. I at last got another blanket and mounted my pony, my guard tying me on hard and fast. So we started out of Marshall, they leading my horse. When daylight came, they untied my legs and allowed me to guide the little black pony. If you had met our party that day, you would have seen a small white man about 45 years old, who was a captain of police named Stokes, a middle-weight dark-looking man, one-fourth Negro, one-fourth Mexican, and one-half white, the former riding a large bay horse, the latter a fine sorrel mare and leading a small black pony with a boy 17 years old tied thereon and shivering with cold. They tried to frighten me every way they could. Stokes said they were going to shoot me if I tried to run off, and said that Jim Smolly would kill me any moment he told him to do so. I, of course, talked very humbly, was full of morality and religion and was strictly down on lawlessness of all kinds. I tried to convince them that I was not an outlaw and did not wish to escape anywhere. When we got to the Sabine River, it was booming and we had to swim. They tied me on again and put a rope around my pony's neck. Stokes leading, me next, and Smolly bringing up the rear. The little black pony could swim like a duck, and with the exception of getting thoroughly wet and cold, we got over all right.

We went on two miles out from the river and stopped for the night. Jim went to get some wood and fodder for our horses, while Capt. Stokes and myself started a fire and struck camp. We went to a house about 100 yards off and got an axe. We came back and he told me to cut some pine from an old pine tree. I assented, but made a complete failure with the axe as I was afraid my pistol might show. Jim soon got back, however, and we made a big fire, fed the horses, got supper, laid down, and slept till morning, when we again started on our road to Waco.

When we reached the Trinity, we found it out of its banks and dangerous to cross. We got the ferryman to ferry us over the main stream, but when we began to cross the bottoms and the sloughs, they tied me on the black pony again and kept me tied until we reached dry land. We went forward again and traveled until night, when we stopped and camped. Capt. Stokes went to get some corn and fodder

31

for our horses. While he was gone, Jim Smolly cursed me, as was his habit, and threatened to shoot me, pointing his pistol at me to scare me. Then he sat down on a stump near our horses, which were hitched to the body of the tree. I pretended to be crying and got behind the little black pony. I put my head down on his back and meanwhile I untied the string that held my pistol. I kept one eye on him to see if he was watching me. When I got the pistol ready, I rushed around on Jim and said, "Throw up your hands." He commenced to draw his pistol when I fired, and Jim Smolly fell dead, killed because he did not have sense enough to throw up his hands at the point of a pistol. I rode Jim Smolly's sorrel mare and rode to Mount Calm that night to my father's. Father gave me another horse and sent the sorrel mare back. This was in January, 1871.

I left my father's soon, bound for Mexico. I was going by way of San Antonio, but was arrested between Belton and Waco by men calling themselves the police. They said they were going to take me to Austin, but night coming on, we stopped about ten miles from Belton. They agreed that one Smith should stand guard, a man named Jones, second, and one Davis the last watch. They had a good deal of whisky with them, and they all got about half drunk: I had concluded to escape on the first opportunity, so when we laid down, I noticed where they put their shooting irons. I did not intend to sleep, but watched for a chance to liberate myself from unlawful arrest.

Jones soon dropped off to sleep and Davis soon followed. Smith sat up to guard me, but he forgot he was on duty or else was unconscious of the danger that threatened him and his companions. He began to nod, but once in a while he would roll his eyes around on me. Pretty soon he put his elbow on his knee and began to snore. I picked up Davis' shotgun and Jones' six-shooter. I fired at Smith's head and then turned the other barrel on Jones at once. As Davis began to arise and inquire what was the matter, I began to work on him with the six-shooter. He begged and hollered, but I kept on shooting until I was satisfied he was dead.

Thus I got back my liberty and my pistols. I took an oath right there never to surrender at the muzzle of a gun. I never have done so, either, although I have been forced through main strength to give up several times since.

I went back by way of Marlin, in Falls County, to tell them all good-bye once more. I told my father what I had done and how those three men had arrested me while I was asleep. He said, "Son, never tell this to mortal man. I don't believe you, but go to Mexico, and go at once. I will go part of the way with you."

I slept in the cellar that night and stayed in an old outhouse the next day. I started the next night and we went through Waco. This was about the 12th of January, 1871. My father went on with me as far as Belton, and there we parted. I went on through Georgetown, through Austin, and thence through Lockhart to Gonzales. I had some relatives in the latter town, and I concluded to stop over and see them.

These were the Clements: Jim, Manning, Joe, Gip, Mary Jane, and Minerva. The girls were both married, the eldest to Jim Denson, the youngest to Ferd Brown. They lived almost directly on my way from Gonzales to Hellena; an old and honored citizen showed me the way to my relatives' home. My guide's name was Jim Cone. I told my relatives I was in trouble and on my way to Mexico. They told me I could go to Kansas with cattle and make some money and at the same time be free from arrest. I therefore concluded to give up my Mexican trip and went to work helping them gather cattle. We gathered mostly for Jake Johnson and Columbus Carol, who were then putting up herds for Kansas.

I thus soon got acquainted with the country on the Sandies, on Elm and Rocky, and on the Guadalupe.

I had not been there long before the boys took me to a Mexican camp where they were dealing monte. I soon learned the rudiments of the game and began to bet with the rest. Finally I turned a card down and tapped the game. My card came and I said, "Pay the queen." The dealer refused. I struck him over the head with my pistol as he was drawing a knife, shot another as he also was drawing a knife. Well, this broke up the monte game and the total casualties were a Mexican with his arm broken, another shot through the lungs, and another with a very sore head. We all went back to camp and laughed about the matter, but the game broke up for good and the Mexican camp was abandoned. The best people of the vicinity said I did a good thing. This was in February, 1871.

When we were gathering cattle for the trail, I was in charge of the herd with strict orders to let no one go into the herd. A Negro named Bob King came to the herd, rode in, and commenced to cut out cattle without permission. I rode up and asked him by whose permission he was cutting cattle in that herd. He said he did not have to have permission and asked who was the boss.

I said, "I am the man."

"Well," he said, "I have come to cut this herd."

"I told him to keep out of it; that Clements would be here directly." He rode right into that herd and cut out a big beef steer. So I rode up to him and struck him over the head with my pistol and told him to get out of my herd. Although he had a six-shooter, he did not do anything, but begged my pardon.

34

About the last of February we got all our cattle branded and started for Abilene, Kansas, about the 1st of March. Jim Clements and I were to take these 1,200 head of cattle up to Abilene and Manning; Gip and Joe Clements were to follow with a herd belonging to Doc Burnett. Jim and I were getting $150 per month.

Nothing of importance happened until we got to Williamson County, where all the hands caught the measles except Jim and myself. We camped about two miles south of Corn Hill and there we rested up and recruited. I spent the time doctoring my sick companions, cooking, and branding cattle.

About the fourth day we were there near Barnett Young's (a relative of mine) a big white steer of the neighborhood gave me considerable trouble. I could not keep him out of the herd, so I pulled my .45 and shot him, aiming to shoot him in the nose, but instead hit him in the eye. That ox gave me no more trouble, but his owner gave me no end of trouble in the courts. I think that ox cost me about $200.

After resting there about ten days, all the hands recovered from the measles, and the cattle and horses having improved so much in flesh, we again started north.

After several weeks of travel we crossed Red River at a point called Red River Station, or Bluff, north of Montague County. We were now in the Indian country and two white men had been killed by Indians about two weeks before we arrived at the town. Of course, all the talk was Indians and everybody dreaded them. We were now on what is called the Chisom [sic] Trail and game of all kinds abounded: buffalo, antelope, and other wild animals too numerous to mention. There were a great many cattle driven that year from Texas. The day we crossed Red River about fifteen herds had crossed, and of course we

35

intended to keep close together going through the Nation for our mutual protection. The trail was thus one line of cattle and you were never out of sight of a herd. I was just about as much afraid of an Indian as I was of a coon. In fact, I was anxious to meet some on the warpath.

There were lots of wolves in that country and I never heard anything like their howling. We killed a beef one night and they made the night hideous. I wanted to capture one, and in the early morning saddled my horse to see if I could not rope or kill one. I struck out from camp and saw a big loafer about 200 yards from camp. He was about 200 yards away, but I turned Roan loose and, pulling my pistol, I commenced shooting. My very first shot hit him in his hip. I ran on to him and roped him. I pulled him to the camp, but the boys said that no wolf could enter camp and shot my rope in two. Mr. Wolf, however, ran the gauntlet and escaped. The whole outfit caught the wolf fever, which resulted in tired men and crippled horses. I also killed some antelope, running on them and shooting them from the saddle.

One morning on the South Canadian River I went out turkey hunting and killed as fine a gobbler as I ever saw. I went over to where he fell, picked him up, and started for my pony. It was just about daylight, and when I got close to my pony, I saw he was snorting and uneasy. I looked in the direction that he seemed afraid of, and about twenty yards off I saw an Indian in the very act of letting fly an arrow at me, and quick as thought, I drew my pistol and fired at him. The ball hit him squarely in the forehead and he fell dead without a groan. I got away from there with my turkey as quickly as I could, went to camp, and we all went to see a dead Indian. The boys wanted to take his bow and arrows as trophies, but I objected. We got a spade and

36

an axe and dug a grave and buried the Indian with his bows and arrows, covering the grave with leaves to hide the spot from other Indians.

These Indians had established a custom of taxing every herd that went through the Nation 10 cents per head. Several other herds joined with us in refusing to pay this, and we never did, though many times it looked like war.

When we were crossing into Kansas, somewhere near Bluff Creek, we were attacked by a band of Osage Indians, who would ride into the herd and cut out little bunches of cattle, sometimes as many as fifteen or twenty head at one time. It was straight-out robbery, and I told the hands to shoot the first Osage that cut another cow.

One morning these Indians came to our camp while I was away and scared the cook and hands almost to death. They took off everything they wanted to, including a fancy silver bridle of mine. I got back to camp about 10 A.M., and when I found out what had happened, you bet I was hot. In a little while about twenty bucks came to the herd, rode in, and commenced to cut out cattle. I rode up to where they were and saw a big Indian using my fancy silver bridle. I asked him how much he would take for it and offered him $5. He grunted an assent and gave me the bridle. When I got it, I told him that was my bridle and someone had stolen it from camp that morning. He frowned and grunted and started to get the bridle back, trying to pull it off my horse. I "jabbed" him with my pistol, and when this would not stop him, I struck him over the head with it. He fell back and yelled to his companions. This put the devil in them. They came up in a body and demanded cattle again. I told them "no" as I had done before. An Indian rode into the herd and cut out a big beef steer. I told him to get out of the herd and pulled my pistol to emphasize my remarks. He was armed and drew his, saying that if I did not let him cut the beef out, he would kill the animal. I told him that if he killed the animal, I would kill him. Well, he killed the beef and I killed him. The other Indians promptly vanished. If they hadn't, there would have been more dead Indians around that herd. The beef he had killed lay dead on the trail, so I mounted him by tying the dead Indian on his back and drove on.

When we had crossed into Kansas, we felt better and safer. On reaching a place called Cow House, about twenty miles on this side of Wichita, a party of men interested in changing the trail from Wichita came out to the herd and induced us to go to the left of Wichita and cross the river about twelve miles above. They wished us to open this trail, as they were interested in building up a new town on the north bank of the Arkansas River. We followed a plough furrow on this new trail and these men furnished a guide. When we had crossed the river, a delegation from the new town came out to meet us and invited all those that could leave the cattle to enjoy the hospitalities of the new town.

About sixty cowboys went to that town and it is needless to say filled up on wine, whisky, etc., some getting rather full. We all came back to the herd in a little while and started out again for Abilene.

We were now on the Newton prairie, and my herd was right in front of a herd driven by Mexicans. This Mexican herd kept crowding us so closely that at last it took two or three hands to keep the Mexican cattle from getting into my herd. The boss Mexican got mad at me for holding, as he said, his cattle back. I told him to turn to the outside of the trail, as he did not have to follow me. This made him all the madder. He fell back from the front of his herd and quit leading the cattle. The result of this was that, no one being in front of them, they rushed right into my herd, so I turned them off to the left. The boss Mexican rode back up to where I was and cursed me in Mexican. He said he would kill me with a sharp-shooter as quick as he could get it from the wagon. In about five minutes I saw him coming back with a gun. He rode up to within about 100 yards of me, got down off his horse, took deliberate aim at me, and fired. The ball grazed my head, going through my hat and knocking it off. He tried to shoot again, but something got wrong with his gun and he changed it to his left hand and pulled his pistol with his right. He began to advance on me, shooting at the same time. He called up his crowd of six or seven Mexicans. In the meanwhile, Jim Clements, hearing that I was in a row, had come to my assistance. I was riding a fiery gray horse and the pistol I had was an old cap and ball, which I had worn out shooting on the trail. There was so much play between the cylinder and the barrel that it would not burst a cap or fire unless I held the cylinder with one hand and pulled the trigger with the other. I made several unsuccessful attempts to shoot the advancing Mexican from my horse but failed. I then got down and tried to shoot and hold my horse, but failed in that, too. Jim Clements shouted at me to "turn that horse loose and hold the cylinder." I did so and fired at the Mexican, who was now only ten paces from me. I hit him in the thigh and stunned him a little. I tried to fire again, but snapped. The Mexican had evidently fired his last load, so we both rushed together in a hand-to-hand fight. The other Mexicans had by this time come close up and were trying to shoot me every chance they got. Jim Clements, seeing I had no show to win, rushed between me and the other Mexicans and told them not to shoot, but to separate us as we were both drunk and did not know what we were doing. Another Mexican who had not been there at the beginning of the fight then rode up and fired two shots at me, but missed. We covered him with our pistols and he stopped. It was then agreed to stop the fight for a time, so the Mexicans went back to their herd. We were not fixed for that fight but wanted to be for the coming one. I had only an old worn-out cap-and-ball pistol and Jim Clements could not fight because his pistol was not loaded. This was the real reason we made a truce for the time. Jim and I went straight to camp and loaded two of the best pistols there. While we were doing this, a message came from the Mexicans that time was up and they were coming. We, of course, sent the messenger back and told the Mexicans to keep off our herd and not to come around; that we did not want any more trouble.

Seven of them gathered on the west side of the herd and seemed to talk matters over. Presently the boss, Hosea, my old foe, with three men, came around to the east side where we were. I had changed horses, so I rode to meet him. He fired at me when about seventy-five yards away, but missed me. I concluded to charge him and turn my horse loose at him, firing as I rode. The first ball did the work. I shot him through the heart and he fell over the horn of his saddle, pistol in hand and one in the scabbard, the blood pouring from his mouth. In an instant I had his horse by the reins and Jim Clements had relieved him of his pistols and Hosea fell dead to the ground. The other Mexicans kept shooting at us, but did not charge. They were in two parties, one about 75 yards to the south, the other about 150 yards to the west. We charged the first party and held our fire until we got close to them. They never weakened, but kept shooting at us all the time. When we got right on

THE FIGHT WITH THE MEXICAN HERDERS

them and opened up, they turned their horses, but we were in the middle of them, dosing them with lead. They wheeled and made a brave stand. We were too quick for them, however, in every way, and they could not go our gait. A few more bullets quickly and rightly placed silenced the party forever. The other party was now advancing on us and shooting as they came. We therefore determined to stampede the herd, which we did in short order by shooting a steer in the nose. This seemed to demoralize them for a while, and they all broke to the cattle except one, who stood still and continued to use his pistol. We cross-fired on him and I ended his existence by putting a ball through his temples. We then took after the rest, who now appeared to be hunting protection from other herders. We caught up with two of them, and Jim Clements covered and held them while I rounded in two more. These latter two said they had nothing to do with the fight and that their companions must have been drunk. We let these two go to the cattle. A crowd of cowmen from all around had now gathered. I suppose there were twenty-five of them around the two Mexicans we had first rounded up. We thus had good interpreters, and once we thought the matter was settled with them, when suddenly the Mexicans, believing they "had the drop," pulled their pistols and both fired point blank at me. I don't know how they missed me. In an instant I fired first at one, then at the other. The first I shot through the heart and he dropped dead. The second I shot through the lungs and Jim shot him too. He fell off his horse, and I was going to shoot him again when he begged and held up both hands. I could not shoot a man, not even a treacherous Mexican, begging and down. Besides, I knew he would die anyway. In comparing notes after the fight, we agreed that I had killed five out of the six dead Mexicans.

Nothing of interest happened until we reached North Cottonwood, where we went into camp to deliver our cattle. We were now about 35 miles from Abilene, Kansas, and it was about the 1st of June that we all got word to come into Abilene, draw our pay, and be discharged.

I have seen many fast towns, but I think Abilene beat them all. The town was filled with sporting men and women, gamblers, cowboys, desperadoes, and the like. It was well supplied with bar rooms, hotels, barber shops, and gambling houses, and everything was open.

Before I got to Abilene, I had heard much talk of Wild Bill, who was then marshal of Abilene. He had a reputation as a killer. I knew Ben Thompson and Phil Coe were there and had met both these men in Texas. Besides these, I learned that there were many other Texans there, and so, although there was a reward offered for me, I concluded to stay some time there, as I knew that Carol and Johnson, the owners of my herd, "squared" me with the officials. When we went to town and settled up, Jim Clements insisted on going home, although they offered him $140 per month to stay. I continued in their employ to look after their stray cattle at $150 per month. Thus we settled our business and proceeded to take in the town.

Columbus Carol got into a fuss with a policeman that night at a notorious resort. Carson was the policeman's name, and he drew a pistol on Carol. I was present and drew mine on Carson, making him leave the place. I told him not to turn his head until he got to the corner of the next street and to go and get Wild Bill, his chief, and come back, and we would treat him likewise. But "they never came back."

Next morning Carol and myself met Carson and Wild Bill on the streets, but nothing happened.

Jim Clements took the train and went back to Texas. Phil Coe and Ben Thompson at that time were running the Bull's Head saloon and gambling hall. They had a big bull painted outside the saloon as a sign, and the city council objected to this for some special reason. Wild Bill, the marshal, notified Ben Thompson and Phil Coe to take the sign down or change it somewhat. Phil Coe thought the ordinance all right, but it made Thompson mad. Wild Bill, however, sent up some painters and materially changed the offending bovine.

For a long time everybody expected trouble between Thompson and Wild Bill, and I soon found out that they were deadly enemies. Thompson tried to prejudice me every way he could against Bill, and told me how Bill, being a Yankee, always picked out Southern men to kill, and especially Texans. I told him, "I am not doing anybody's fighting just now except my own, but I know how to stick to a friend. If Bill needs killing, why don't you kill him yourself?"

He said, "I would rather get someone else to do it."

I told him then that he had struck the wrong man. I had not yet met Bill Heycox, but really wished for a chance to have a set-to with him just to try his luck.

One night in a wine room he was drinking with some friends of mine when he remarked that he would like to have an introduction to me. George Johnson introduced us, and we had several glasses of wine together. He asked me all about the fight on the Newton prairie and showed me a proclamation from Texas offering a reward for my arrest. He said, "Young man, I am favorably impressed with you, but don't let Ben Thompson influence you; you are in enough trouble now, and if I can do you a favor, I will do it."

44

I was charmed with his liberal views, and told him so. We parted friends.

I spent most of my time in Abilene in the saloons and gambling houses, playing poker, faro, and seven-up. One day I was rolling ten pins and my best horse was hitched outside in front of the saloon. I had two six-shooters on, and, of course, I knew the saloon people would raise a row if I did not pull them off. Several Texans were there rolling ten pins and drinking. I suppose we were pretty noisy. Wild Bill came in and said we were making too much noise and told me to pull off my pistols until I got ready to go out of town. I told him I was ready to go now, but did not propose to put up my pistols, go or no go. He went out and I followed him. I started up the street when someone behind me shouted out, "Set up. All down but nine."

Wild Bill whirled around and met me. He said, "What are you howling about, and what are you doing with those pistols on?"

I said, "I am just taking in the town."

He pulled his pistol and said, "Take those pistols off. I arrest you."

I said all right and pulled them out of the scabbard, but while he was reaching for them, I reversed them and whirled them over on him with the muzzles in his face, springing back at the same time. I told him to put his pistols up, which he did. I cursed him for a long-haired scoundrel that would shoot a boy with his back to him (as I had been told he intended to do me). He said, "Little Arkansaw, you have been wrongly informed."

I shouted, "This is my fight and I'll kill the first man that fires a gun."

Bill said, "You are the gamest and quickest boy I ever saw. Let us compromise this matter and I will be your friend. Let us go in here and take a drink, as I want to talk to you and give you some advice."

At first I thought he might be trying to get the drop on me, but he finally convinced me of his good intentions, and we went in and took a drink. We went into a private room and I had a long talk with him and we came out friends.

I had been drinking pretty freely that day and towards night went into a restaurant to get something to eat. A man named Pain was with me, a Texan who had just come up the trail. While we were in the restaurant several drunken men came in and began to curse Texans. I said to the nearest one, "I'm a Texan."

He began to curse me and threatened to slap me over. To his surprise I pulled my pistol, and he promptly pulled his. At the first fire he jumped behind my friend Pain, who received the ball in his only arm. He fired one shot and ran but I shot at him as he started, the ball hitting him in the mouth, knocking out several teeth and coming out behind his left ear. I rushed outside, pistol in hand, and jumped over my late antagonist, who was lying in the doorway. I met a policeman on the sidewalk, but I threw my pistol in his face and told him to "hands up." He did it.

I made my way to my horse and went north to Cottonwood, about 35 miles, to await results. While I was there, a Mexican named Bideno shot and killed Billy Coran, a cowman who had come up the trail with me. He was bossing a herd then, holding it near-by Abilene for the market. His murder by this Mexican was a most foul and treacherous one, and although squad after squad tried to arrest this Mexican, they never succeeded in either killing or arresting him.

Many prominent cowmen came to me and urged me to follow the murderer. I consented if they would go to Abilene and get a warrant for him. They did so, and I was appointed a deputy sheriff and was given letters of introduction to cattlemen whom I should meet. About sunrise on the 27th of June, 1871, I left the North Cottonwood with Jim Rodgers to follow Bideno. Of course, we proposed to change horses whenever we wanted to. This was easy to do, as there were many horses around the herds and we knew they would let us have them when we explained our purpose. We hoped to catch up with him before he got to the Nation, and specially before he got to Texas. Off we went in a lope and got to Newton, about 50 miles away, by 4 P.M. I had learned of a herd there bossed by a brother of the dead Billy Coran, and I sent a messenger to him, telling him (the messenger) not to spare horseflesh. Coran came and one Anderson with him. I told him of his brother's death, and we were soon on the trail with fresh horses and four instead of two in our party.

We had not as yet heard one word from Bideno. We expected to reach Wichita that night. About twelve miles from Newton, just about dusk, we came upon a herd bossed by Ben McCulloch, who was afterwards assistant superintendent of the Huntsville Penitentiary, while I was there. We changed horses again and took the trail, having as yet heard nothing of Bideno. We reached Wichita about 11 o'clock that night, having traveled 100 miles since starting. We concluded to rest until morning and then go on the south side of the river and make inquiry. I knew there were several Mexican herds near the river which Bideno might have gone to for a change of horses. We went next morning to these herds, going from one to the other, hunting for information. Finally we struck a Mexican who said that just such a man had stayed at his camp about 10 o'clock last night and had traded horses with one of his men early

47

in the morning. He said the horse he had traded for was the best in camp. We were convinced that this must have been Bideno, so changing horses and flushed with hope, we hit the trail again about 7 A.M. in a long lope.

We saw a herder about 8 o'clock who told us that two hours before he had seen a Mexican wearing a broad-brimmed hat and going south in a lope, keeping about 200 yards from the trail. We were now satisfied we were on the right track and pulled out again, expecting to change horses at Cow House Creek, about 15 miles further on. We met a man near Cow House who told us that he had seen a Mexican wearing a broad-brimmed hat and going south in a lope. When we got to Cow House, we changed our horses at once and found that Bideno had done likewise an hour before. It was now about 10 o'clock, and hoping to overtake him before we got to Bluff Creek, 25 miles off, on the line of Arkansas and the Indian Territory, we pushed our fresh horses to a fast lope. We heard from him several times, but he was always in a lope and always off the road.

After going about 20 miles, we again changed horses, so that if we ran up on him, our horses would be fresh. When we got to within two miles of Bluff Creek, the road forked. Anderson and I went through the city, while Rodgers and Coran took the other fork, all agreeing to meet in the Indian Nation on the other side of the creek.

Anderson and I, before going far, got direct information that Bideno had just unsaddled his horse and had gone up town inquiring for a restaurant. We fired off our pistols and by this means got Coran and Rodgers to hear us and come back.

We soon got to Bluff, which was a town of about 50 houses. There were some bar rooms and restaurants in a line, and we agreed to ride up like cowboys, hitch our horses, and divide into two parties, each going into different places. Anderson and I went into a restaurant, but before we reached it, we had to go into a saloon. I called for the drinks and took in the situation. I asked if we could get dinner and if a Mexican herder was eating dinner back there. They said there was; so I told my partner to get out his gun and follow me. We stepped into the entrance, and I recognized Bideno. With my pistol by my side I said, "Bideno, I am after you; surrender; I do not wish to hurt you, and you shall not be hurt while you are in my hands."

He was sitting at the table eating and shook his head and frowned. He then dropped his knife and fork and grabbed his pistol. As he did it, I told him to throw up his hands.

When he got his pistol out, I fired at him across the table and he fell over a dead man, the ball hitting him squarely in the center of the forehead.

Hearing the firing, Coran and Rodgers rushed in also. Coran said, "I just want to shoot my brother's murderer one time. Is he dead?"

I told him he was, but he wanted to shoot him anyway. I would not let him, but he took his hat as a trophy.

In the meantime the waiter was jumping up and down, begging us not to kill him; that he was a friend of cowboys, etc. I quieted him by telling him if he did not get out, he might, perhaps, get shot accidently, and he promptly acted on my suggestion.

We all went into the saloon, and the bartender said, "Take what you want." We took some good whisky and he would not let us pay for it.

Quite a crowd had collected by this time, and they all wanted to know what the shooting was about. I got outside the saloon and told the crowd how this Mexican had murdered a prominent cowman on the 26th at North Cotton-

49

wood; how we had followed him and demanded his surrender; how he had refused to give up and had drawn his pistol, when I was forced to shoot him. I then introduced John Coran, the dead man's brother. They all commended our actions, and I gave those people $20 to bury him.

We started back to Abilene, rejoicing over our good luck. We reached Wichita that night, which was about 50 miles away. As we had ridden about 150 miles in 36 hours, we all rested that night in Wichita.

There I told my companions my troubles in Abilene. We all agreed to go to Newton and thence to Abilene, where they were to stick to me against anything.

I had heard that Wild Bill had said that if I ever came back to Abilene, he would kill me, so I had determined to go back there and if Bill tried to arrest me, to kill him.

Well, we stopped next at Newton and took in that town in good style. The policemen tried to hold us down, but they all resigned—I reckon. We certainly shut up that town.

We went on to Abilene, fearing nothing but God. While we were opening wine there, Wild Bill came in and asked me if I remembered our talk in the "Apple Jack."

"Well," said he, "you can not 'hurrah' me, and I am not going to have it."

I told him, "I don't wish to hurrah you; but I have come to stay, regardless of you."

"Well," he said, "you can stay and wear your guns, but those other fellows must pull them off. You are in no danger here. I congratulate you on getting your Mexican. Come in and invite your friends. We will open a bottle of wine."

The boys had been watching us pretty closely, and we all went into a room, they having their guns on. The marshal said nothing about their pistols then and, after drinking a couple of bottles of wine, left.

I then told my companions that Bill was my friend and had asked me to see that they took their pistols off. They asked me why I did not pull mine off. I told them that the marshal had not demanded that of me, but I knew he was our friend and would protect us all, and if he did not, I would. Well, they said that if Wild Bill was all right with me, they would go home, which they did.

Everybody in Abilene wanted to see the man that killed the murderer of Billy Coran, and I received substantial compliments in the shape of $20, $50, and $100 bills. I did not want to take the money at first, but I finally concluded there was nothing wrong about it, so took it as a proof of their friendship and gratitude for what I had done. I think I got about $400 in that way. Besides this, some wealthy cowmen made up a purse and gave me $600, so altogether I got about $1,000 for my work. I wish to say, however, that at the time I killed him I never expected to receive a cent, and only expected to have my expenses paid.

It was about the 2nd of July that John Coran, Jim Rodgers, Hugh Anderson, and myself parted at Abilene. In a day or two Manning and Gip Clements came into Abilene and hunted me up. They found me with Jake Johnson and Frank Bell. To celebrate the meeting, we opened several bottles of wine, and then Manning said, "Wes, I want to see you privately."

He, Gip, and myself went up to my private room. Manning said, "Wes, I killed Joe and Dolph Shadden last night, but I was justified."

"Well," said I, "I am glad you are satisfied, but I would stick to you all the same, even if you were not satisfied with your action."

51

Manning said that he was bossing a herd for Doc Burnett in Gonzales county and was driving them here. He had selected his own hands and had hired these Shadden boys. Everything had gone on smoothly until they crossed Red River. Then the Shaddens commenced playing off and refused to go on night duty. When they were ordered to do so, they became insulting and demanded their time and money. When told they could quit they wanted pay for all the time they had gone through to Abilene. This Manning refused to do, but offered to pay them for the time they had actually worked. He told them it was either this or leave camp or do night duty and stay. They stayed and did night duty. All the time going through the Nation, they were trying to make the other hands dissatisfied and told them that they intended to kill Manning before they got to Abilene, where they knew that Jim Clements and Wes Hardin were and they would take Manning's part, of course.

When they crossed the Canadian, they gave up work entirely. Manning then offered them their full pay if they would leave. This they would not do, so he told Gip and the rest of the hands to watch them in word and actions. Manning actually would stay away from camp at nights to avoid trouble, as he knew they were fixing to kill him there. They began to talk about his cowardice in sleeping away from camp at nights. When the herd crossed the Arkansas, Manning told a friend of his that had their confidence, too, that he was not going to sleep out of camp any longer.

The Shadden boys then said, "Well, if he comes back to sleep in camp at night, we will kill him."

Manning was told of their intention and told his brother Gip in their presence to make down his bed in a certain place, which he did.

When they had gone, Manning told Gip what was up.

Manning went on duty first that night himself, and a hand came out to the herd and begged him not to go back to camp that night as these Shadden boys were sitting up waiting to kill him. Manning, however, took a friend and went to camp. He got there later than they expected and called out in a loud voice, "Gip, get up and go on herd." Gip said, "all right." Joe Shadden jumped up with his pistol, but Manning had on a slicker and also had his pistol in his hand. Manning fired first and put a bullet through Joe's head. Dolph, meanwhile, had fired at Manning, the ball going through his slicker and vest. Manning and Dolph Shadden then rushed together and scuffled, but Manning managed to fire, shooting him through the breast. He fell back on his bed, telling Manning he had killed him. Manning then turned the herd over to one of his hands, got his young brother Gip, and came on here. When Manning told me this, I said, "I have had a heap of trouble, but I stand square in Abilene. Wild Bill is my particular friend, and he is the one to help you here if papers come from Texas for you. Now, Manning, pull off your pistols until I see Bill and fix him." I made Gip do the same thing. I then saw Columbus Carol and Jake Johnson, and it was agreed that Columbus should see Wild Bill and square Manning Clements. But, unfortunately, Columbus got drunk and squared nothing. That evening we all dropped into a gambling hall and began to buck at monte. Wild Bill came in and said, "Hello, little Arkansaw." I said, "Hello yourself; how would you like to be called Hello!" Bill bought $20 worth of checks and lost them. Then he bought $50 and then $100. Manning and I walked out and went over to the American House to get supper. I had finished eating, but Manning and Gip had not, when in walked Wild Bill and McDonald. I knew in an instant that they had come to arrest Manning.

Bill gave me the wink. In a few minutes he said, "How did you come out?" I told him about $25 ahead and asked him what he did. "I lost $250," said he. I told him I knew all the time he was playing the house's money when we had left. He laughed and said yes, that those fellows knew better than to refuse him. By this time Manning had finished eating and Wild Bill said, "Are you through eating?"

Manning told him "yes," and he said: "I suppose you name is Clements. I have a telegram here to arrest Manning

MANNING CLEMENTS

Clements; so consider yourself under arrest." Manning said "all right." I told Bill to let McDonald guard his prisoner a moment and told Bill I wanted to speak to him privately. I asked him if Columbus Carol had posted him.

"No," said he, "he is drunk. Why did you not post me yourself?"

I then told him that he had once promised to do any favor I asked of him; that Manning was a cousin of mine and that he relied on me for safety. I then asked Wild Bill what I could expect from him. He told me he would turn him loose. I told him that was the only way of avoiding trouble. It was agreed that he should protect himself and his reputation as an officer by taking Manning to the Bull's Head Saloon (Phil Coe's) and from thence to the lock-up. I asked him to tell me exactly what time he would turn him out, and he said "12 o'clock." I then called Manning in and told him that Columbus had gotten drunk and had not posted Wild Bill and that in order to protect Wild Bill he must go to jail, but would be turned out at 12 M.

Wild Bill and McDonald then took Manning to jail, while I went to Jess McCoy and bought a horse and saddle for Manning to ride. By this time they had landed him in jail, and Bill had sent for me to come up town. Jake Johnson was cutting up about the arrest and had a band of 25 Texans ready to liberate him. The police were also gathering at the jail. I took Jake off and told him that Columbus had gotten drunk and had not posted Bill. I explained it all to him and told him to bring his men up to Phil Coe's saloon and stay there. I went up to Phil Coe's and privately agreed to break open the jail at 12 o'clock if Wild Bill did not turn him loose at the appointed time. We went to work then and got 50 good men, stationing them in the back of the Bull's Head Saloon, just across the street from the jail. I told Phil Coe that Wild Bill and I had agreed to meet at 8 o'clock to make a run or take the town in, so to speak. and it might be possible that I would not see him again before the play. I told Phil Coe that Wild Bill and I had set our watches together, and so he and I also set ours together. I agreed with Phil that he should get the key by

10 minutes to 12, and if at that time he had not gotten it, to send me word. I told him where Wild Bill and I would be exactly at that time. I told him if I did not get word from him by 5 minutes to 12, I would kill Wild Bill, but whether he heard shooting or not to break open the jail if he did not get the key. At 10 minutes to 8 by my watch, I went to meet Wild Bill, and we commenced to take in the gambling houses, etc. We began on monte, and the banks we did not break, closed. Then we tried faro, and after a while they closed, too. Bill played the bluff racket and I bet with him, so where they paid him they had to pay me as well. I think we won about $1,000 apiece that night. On going over town, we learned that a policeman named Tom Carson had arrested some female friends of ours and we determined to see them turned loose and to whip Tom Carson, although he was chief deputy of Wild Bill. We went to the calaboose and met Carson, but Bill did not say anything to him then, and called to the turnkey to bring the key. The prisoners got a hack and went home rejoicing. Tom Carson asked Wild Bill what he did it for, and Bill answered his question by knocking him down and then jumping on him with both feet. It was a bad beating up, for Wild Bill was a man 6 feet high and weighed 200 pounds. He was light complexioned, blue eyed, and his hair hung down his shoulders in yellow curls. He was a brave, handsome fellow, but somewhat overbearing. He had fine sense and was a splendid judge of human nature. After this we again went up town, and directly I asked Bill what time it was. He said, "15 minutes to 12," and handed me the key wrapped up in a piece of paper. I sent it at once to Phil Coe's at the Bull Head Saloon and sent word where Manning could find me. Manning soon joined me; we had some wine and then went to our horses.

LAST BREAK IN ABILENE

We rode to Smoky River, where we got down and talked matters over. I had provided him with money and everything else necessary for the trip. It was agreed that we should meet again at Barnett Hardin's in Hill County, Texas, and that I should take care of his younger brother, Gip, whom he left with me. We parted with this understanding, and he went to Texas, while I went back to Abilene, reaching the town about 3 A.M.

In those days my life was constantly in danger from secret or hired assassins, and I was always on the lookout.

On the 7th of July, Gip and I had gone to our rooms in the American Hotel to retire for the night. We soon got to bed, when presently I heard a man cautiously unlock my door and slip in with a big dirk in his hand. I halted him with a shot and he ran; I fired at him again and again, and he fell dead with four bullets in his body. He had carried my pants with him and so I jumped back, slammed the door, and cried out that I would shoot the first man that came in. I had given one of my pistols to Manning the night before, so the one I had was now empty.

Now, I believed that if Wild Bill found me in a defenseless condition, he would take no explanation, but would kill me to add to his reputation. So in my shirt and drawers I told Gip to follow me and went out on the portico.

Just as I got there, a hack drove up with Wild Bill and four policemen. I slipped back and waited until they had gotten well inside the hotel and then jumped off over the hack. Gip came after me.

I sent Gip to a friend of mine to hide him. I hardly knew what to do. I was sleepy in the first place, and without arms or clothes. I knew all the bridges were guarded and the country was out after me, believing that I had killed a man in cold blood, instead of a dirty, low-down, would-be

58

assassin. I concluded to slip around and sleep in a haystack which I knew of. I heard them come and look for me, one remarking that he believed I was in that haystack and started to set it on fire. I crawled away into the haystack, knowing they would not set it on fire because it was too close to a store. If they had done so, you would have seen a lad of 19 years old in his night clothes crawling away from the officers and the fire in a hurry. I crawled to the edge of the stack after a while and saw two squads of police not far off. I crawled to a cornfield in roasting ear, keeping the haystack between me and the police. Presently I saw a lone cowboy riding up within a few yards of me. I asked him if he knew me. He said he did. I put my hand to my side and told him to get down on the other side. He did it and I got up. The police saw this move, and I turned my nag loose. The police were right after me, and we had a hot race to the river, three miles off. I got there a quarter of a mile ahead and plunged my horse in. He swam like a duck and I got across in safety. They fired several shots at me from the other side and their bullets whistled unpleasantly close to me, so I soon put space between myself and pursuers. I went about a mile, when I looked back and saw three men coming at full speed, but I rode on, and at that time few men could outride me. I weighed 155 pounds and was confident in myself, even though I was undressed and unarmed. I let that dun mare go a gait that I thought she could stand and that would put me in camp at least half an hour ahead of my pursuers. I looked back again and could see them coming about four miles off. It was about five miles to camp and down hill the most of the way, so I let her go and made it in about twenty minutes.

I was a sorry spectacle when I got to that camp. I was

bareheaded, unarmed, redfaced, and in my night clothes. I went to work at once to meet my pursuers and got two six-shooters and a Winchester. The cook had prepared dinner, and as I had eaten nothing since the evening before, I certainly relished it. The camp was right on the north bank of North Cottonwood, and I dropped down under the bank while my pursuers rode up. Tom Carson and two others inquired of the cook where I was. He told them I had gone to the herd and asked them to get down and have dinner. When they were eating, I stepped up near them, but not near enough for any of them to grab me. I covered Tom Carson with my Winchester and told them, "All hands up or I'll shoot." All their hands went up, and I told the cook to relieve those gentlemen of their arms and told them that any resistance on their part would mean certain and untimely death. The cook did his work well, and I told them to finish their dinner, while I sat on a dry-goods box with my Winchester in my hands.

When they were through, I made Tom Carson and his two men pull off their clothes, pants, and boots, and sent them all back in this condition to face a July sun for thirty-five miles on a bald prairie.

I waited out on Cottonwood several days until Gip Clements came out.

On the 11th of July, 1871, Gip and I left Cottonwood for Texas, well armed and equipped in every way. We went by Emporia and Parsons and thence into the Nation.

One day we stopped for dinner with a trader who had a wagon drawn by a horse and a mule. He was a rough-looking fellow, heavy set, dark, and weighing about 180 pounds. He professed to be an expert shot and we commenced to shoot for a dollar a shot. In those days I was a crack shot, and I won several dollars. He then challenged me to shoot for $20. I did so and won easily. He then wanted to shoot for $50, which I again did, and he again lost. He increased to $100, which I won. This made him wrathy and he wanted to fight. I told him he couldn't whip me, and he called me a liar, drawing his pistol. I cocked mine in his face, and Gip interfered by catching the trader's pistol, which alone prevented me from shooting him. Gip then took it away from him, and he commenced abusing me and said if Gip would give him back his pistol, he would kill me. Of course, he knew that Gip would not do this. He kept cursing me and told me he could carry weight and whip my sort. I said, "Old man, I don't want to kill you, but you have only yourself to blame if you make me do it."

I guarded him while Gip saddled the horses. All this time he was trying to get to the wagon where his Winchester was, and I had to warn the old fool repeatedly to keep back or I would surely kill him. When Gip got the horses saddled, I made him throw down the Trader's pistol and guard him until I had gotten off about 300 yards. Then Gip bade the Indian trader farewell, and we rode off, laughing, but glad we did not have to kill him.

Nothing of interest happened until we got to Barnett Hardin's on the 30th of July, in Hill County, Texas. There we met Manning Clements, and after staying about a week, we struck out for Gonzales County, where the Clements lived.

We arrived at Manning's house on the 7th of August, 1871. The Shadden brothers, whom Manning had killed, had a brother and a brother-in-law living near there, and we expected trouble, but soon after our arrival they concluded to move out.

E. J. Davis was governor then, and his State Police were

composed of carpet-baggers, scalawags from the North, with ignorant Negroes frequently on the force. Instead of protecting life, liberty, and property, they frequently destroyed it. We all knew that many members of this State Police outfit were members of some secret vigilant band, especially in DeWitt and Gonzales counties. We were all opposed to mob law and so soon became enemies. The consequence was that a lot of Negro police made a raid on me without lawful authority. They went from house to house looking for me and threatening to kill me, and frightening the women and children to death.

They found me at a small grocery store in the southern portion of Gonzales County. I really did not know they were there until I heard some one say, "Throw up your hands or die!"

I said "all right," and turning around saw a big black Negro with his pistol cocked and presented. I said, "Look out, you will let that pistol go off, and I don't want to be killed accidently."

He said, "Give me those pistols."

I said "all right," and handed him the pistols, handle foremost. One of the pistols turned a somerset in my hand and went off. Down came the Negro, with his pistol cocked, and as I looked outside, I saw another Negro on a white mule firing into the house at me. I told him to hold up, but he kept on, so I turned my Colt's .45 on him and knocked him off his mule my first shot. I turned around then to see what had become of No. 1 and saw him sprawling on the floor with a bullet through his head, quivering in blood. I walked out of the back door to get my horse, and when I got back to take in the situation, the big Negro on the white mule was making for the bottom at a 2:40 gait. I tried to head him off, but he dodged and ran into a lake. I afterwards learned that he stayed in there with his nose out of the water until I left. The Negro I killed was named Green Paramoor and the one on the white mule was a blacksmith from Gonzales named John Lackey—in fact, they were both from that town.

News of this, of course, spread like fire, and myself and friends declared openly against Negro or Yankee mob rule and misrule in general. In the meantime the Negroes of Gonzales and adjoining counties had begun to congregate at Gonzales and were threatening to come out to the Sandies and with torch and knife depopulate the entire country. We at once got together about 25 men good and true and sent these Negroes word to come along, that we would not leave enough of them to tell the tale. They had actually started, but some old men from Gonzales talked to them and made them return to their homes. From that time on we had no Negro police in Gonzales. This happened in September, 1871.

Soon after this I took a trip to see some relatives in Brenham, and nothing of interest happened until I returned.

A posse of Negroes from Austin came down after me, and I was warned of their coming. I met them prepared and killed three of them. They returned sadder and wiser. This was in September, 1871.

As my parents were still living in Limestone County at Mount Calm, I concluded to go and see them. I went through Austin, through Georgetown, Belton, and Waco, from thence to Mount Calm, where I found my parents well and glad to see me again. I stayed there until after Christmas and then went to Dallas. Returning to Mount Calm, I stayed there one night and went back south to Gonzales.

I got back the night Gip Clements married Annie Tennille, and I enjoyed the supper and dance very much. My sweetheart, who was soon to be my bride, Jane Bowen, was there.

Nothing of importance happened until I married Jane Bowen, though we were expecting the police to come any time. They would have met with a warm reception in those times, when the marriage bells were ringing all around.

About two months after I married I had some business at King's ranch and went by the way of Goliad and San Patricio to Corpus Christi. At the latter town I stayed several days and then went out to King's ranch (sometimes called San Gertrudas). On my way out there, when about 45 miles from Corpus Christi, I stopped to get my dinner and pulled off my saddle to let my horse graze. I looked around and saw two Mexicans coming towards me. They stopped about 75 yards away, got down, and began to make coffee. This was evidently done to throw me off my guard, but it did not have the desired effect. I just saddled up my horse again and rode on, hoping to lose them. After I had gone about four miles, I saw the same two Mexicans coming to meet me again. When they got about 50 yards away from me, one got on one side of the road and the other on the other side to cross-fire on me. I took them to be robbers, as they were. I spurred my horse out of the road, and they immediately pulled their pistols and started out after me. I suddenly wheeled and fired quickly. I shot the one on my left off his horse, and the one on the right soon quit the fight. Being in a strange country, I put as much space between myself and the robbers as possible. I never did know whether I killed both Mexicans or not.

I was riding a splendid horse and got to Capt. King's ranch that night. I stayed there the next day, transacted my business, and in company with Jim Cox I made my way to San Diego, stayed there overnight, and then with Cox went on to Banquetto and stayed there a day or two.

There I got to thinking that I had one of the prettiest and sweetest girls in the country as my wife, who would soon be looking for me, for I had promised to be gone only twelve days. The more I thought of her the more I wanted to see her. So one night about 10 o'clock I started from Banquetto for Gonzales County, 100 miles away.

I got home at about 4 A.M., but forever ruined a good horse worth $50 in doing so. The sight of my wife recompensed me for the loss of old Bob.

This was in May, and I conceived the idea of going east with a bunch of horses. I commenced to gather them at once, and in two weeks I was ready to go to Louisiana. I bid my angel wife good-bye. It nearly broke my heart, for she had implicit confidence in me and her hope and prayer was my safe return. This was about the 5th of June, 1872.

I concluded to go ahead of the herd to eastern Texas, where I had some relatives. My herd was in charge of Jess and John Harper, who had been raised in Sabine County. Their father was living at Hemphill and was then sheriff of Sabine, so we agreed to meet at Hemphill, or, rather, I agreed to wait for them there.

Nothing unusual happened on the trip except at Willis, where some fellows tried to arrest me for carrying a pistol, but they got the contents thereof instead. I stopped a week at Livingstone and stayed with my Uncle Barnett, Aunt Anne, and my cousins. We all had a splendid time, and then I went to Hemphill about the last of June.

I had a race horse at that time named "Joe," and he was hard to catch on a quarter of a mile. I soon matched a race with some parties from San Augustine in an adjoining county. I think the race was for $250 and we were to run 350 yards. I took Billy Harper and went 25 miles north to their tracks, won the race easily, and got the money without any trouble.

It was now the 20th of July, and expecting the horses soon, Billy Harper and I went back to Hemphill. I waited there for the horses and gambled, as much for past time as for money.

On the 26th of July I got into a difficulty with Sonny Spites, one of E. J. Davis' infamous State Police. It happened in this way: A man named O'Connor, returning from Louisiana, was going back home to Austin and stayed one night near Hemphill. A State Policeman arrested him because he had on a pistol and brought him into Hemphill, where, on the policeman's bare statement the magistrate fined him $25 and costs, besides confiscating his pistol. I heard of the outrage and explained the case to the justice, who granted O'Connor a new trial and acquitted him. In the meantime the policeman had taken possession of O'Connor's horse and saddle and was already trying to sell them to pay the fine and costs, O'Connor being broke. I was in the front of the courthouse talking the matter over with O'Connor and some others when a small boy about 10 years old began abusing Spites for arresting O'Connor at his father's house. Spites came up and listened to him and finally told the boy if he did not shut up he would arrest him, too. The boy ridiculed him and defied him to do it, telling him that no one but a coward would arrest a poor traveler. Spites told him if he did not shut up he would whip him. The boy told him he was not afraid, just to go ahead and whip and arrest him. Spites got up to slap the boy, when I told him to hold on, that if he was in earnest to

66

slap a man. He told me he would arrest me for interfering with him in the discharge of his duty. I told him he could not arrest one side of me, and the boy laughed. Spites started to draw a pistol. I pulled a derringer with my left and my six-shooter with my right and instantly fired with my derringer. The dauntless policeman ran to the courthouse and asked the judge to protect him. I learned afterwards that Judge O. M. Roberts was the man appealed to. I would not shoot a fleeing man, not even a policeman, so I jumped on a horse and rode around to where my own was at Dr. Cooper's. When I got there, Billy Harper was leading my horse Joe out of the stable and Mrs. Cooper was bringing my saddle bags. I saddled Joe as quickly as possible and got my saddle bags on. (Mrs. Cooper was Billy's sister.) She cried out, "Wes, yonder comes pa with some men; for God's sake, don't shoot."

I told them good-bye and to get out of the way. Billy was trying to let down the bars and the sheriff and posse were right on me. I knew the sheriff was my friend, so I would not fire on him. I put spurs to Joe and went over the bars. Just as we went over, two balls struck Joe in the neck, but we soon distanced them and went to a friend's house about two miles from town. I awaited developments there and sent for Billy Harper.

Billy came back about dark and told me that Spites was not mortally wounded, only hit in the shoulder and scared to death. He said everybody approved of what I had done, and that Jess and John Harper had come with the horses. They were at Frank Lewis' with the herd, about seven miles from town, and were expecting me out tomorrow. This was about the 26th day of July, 1872.

On the 27th I went out to the herd and stayed there a few days. I sold my horses to the Harper Bros. and started back to Gonzales County, but expected to stop in Polk and Trinity counties on my way. Nothing unusual happened until I got within ten miles of Livingstone, in Polk County, where I stopped at a store, and there being some gay fellows there, we soon made a race. The race was for $250, $100 being put up as a forfeit, and the distance being a quarter of a mile. The date of the race was the 30th of July. The men I had made the race with were named Hickman, and I was told they intended to take the money whether they won or not. When the time came for me to put up the other $150 with the stake holder, I told him what I had heard. His name was Dick Hudson, and I told him I knew him when we were boys together in Polk County. He said he knew me well, so I told him there was my money, but I wanted the other parties to understand that no man or set of men could take my money without killing me unless they won it; that if these parties wanted a fight instead of a race, they could not commence any too soon to suit me. After Hickman Bros. heard of this, they altered their tone and wanted to draw down, but I would not draw. At 12 o'clock (the time limit for putting up) I claimed and received the $350 without a murmur from the Hickmans.

My uncle, Barnett Hardin, lived only ten miles from there, so I went to his place on the 30th of July and hunted and fished for a week. After this Barnett Jones, a cousin of mine, and I went up into Trinity County, where we had some relatives and friends, getting to Trinity City on the 7th of August. We went to John Gates' saloon and ten pin alley, where I commenced to roll. Everybody beat me for the drinks, and after I had lost a round or two, a man named Phil Sublet and I matched a game for $50 in or out. We were to roll anything we wished, from a pony up. It was to be a ball game at $5 a ball. I beat him six straights and won $30 of the $50. He said, "I am going to take my stake down."

I told him we had made the game for $50, and I reckoned he would have to have my consent first.

He said, "No, by God."

I told him that he could not get it unless the stake holder gave it to him after he had won it. He said I was a g—— d—— liar and put his hand to his pistol. I slapped him in the face and shoved a bull-dog pistol at his head. Friends interfered, and we made peace.

We then rolled another ball apiece and I beat him. Then I told him he could draw down the rest of his stake, Sublet thus having lost $35.

We then went out into the front room, where the bar room was, to have something to drink at my expense. While we were drinking, Sublet slipped off, and I missed him pretty soon. It flashed across my mind that he had gone off to get a gun, so I went behind the counter and got two six-shooters out of my saddle bags. I went to the front window, which opened to the south and was behind the counter. The saloon was a plank structure, 60x70 feet. It faced north and south and was about 20 feet wide. A front door from the south and front formed the entrance to the bar room. The bar counter was on the left as you went in. The bar was cut off from the alley by a partition with a door therein. There was a door that opened into the alley from the east about ten feet from the partition, and also a window opened on the south or front end of the saloon. I was at the window when John Gates, the proprietor, told me to go into the alley, that the fuss between Sublet and I was all fixed up. I reluctantly consented to go back into the bowling alley. When I got there I heard some one shouting out, "Clear the way, I will shoot anyone that interferes with me. Come out, you g—— d—— s—— of a b——."

He was in the street south of the front door and was on his way round to the east door of the alley. I appeared at that door with my pistol, and he fired one barrel of a shotgun at me. I thought I would kill him, but did not want to get into any new trouble so fired at him, not intending to hit him, and stepped back. As I did so, a drunken man got up and caught me by the vest, saying that he and I could whip anybody. He had a big knife in his hand and I told him to turn me loose, but before he did it, he pulled me into the middle or partition door. By this time Sublet had gotten in line with the door, and as we darkened it, he fired the other barrel of his shotgun at me. I knew I was shot, so I instantly took after him with my six-shooter, but he threw down his gun and broke for his life. I ran him through the streets and into a dry-goods store. As he went through the store, I fired at him, but my pistol snapped and I found I had my pistol with the broken cylinder spring. My man was still on the run, and I was getting weak from loss of blood. I fired again as he went out the door and the ball passed through his shoulder. I was getting mighty weak now, but staggered to the door as he ran, hoping to kill the man who I thought had killed me. He was about 75 yards away, and I saw I could never kill him, so I turned to some friends who were near and told them, "I am either killed or shot. If all the gold in the world belonged to me, I would freely give it to kill him. I have one consolation, however, I made the coward run."

By this time my cousin, Barnett Jones, had arrived, and as they were holding me up, I recognized him. I told him to take a belt I had which held about $2,000 in gold; to get my saddle bags, which had about $250 in silver, and give it to my wife in Gonzales County. I told him to tell her that I honestly tried to avoid this trouble, but when I was shot, I ran my foe and made him pull his freight for his life.

Barnett, however, told me not to give up, that they were going to do all they could do for me, and that they would bring me to Dr. Carrington's office. The doctor called in another doctor, who, after examining me, decided to take the balls out. Two buckshot had struck me a little to the left of the navel. They had passed through my right kidney and had lodged between my backbone and ribs. Two others had struck my belt buckle, which was a big silver one, and that was what saved me. The doctors asked me if I thought I could stand the operation without opiates. I told them yes, that if I died I wanted my head clear. They placed me on my face and went to work with knife and forceps. They soon had the two buckshot out of me.

Dr. Carrington then told me that my wounds, ordinarily speaking, were fatal, but if I would be submissive, there was a chance for me. I told him I would take that chance and obey his orders. Everybody thought I would die. I told my friends to cut the wires so that they could not send any papers from Austin for me. They placed me in an hotel and gave me the best of treatment.

About the 15th of August I was told that I had to move or be arrested. I had never gotten up out of bed, but the doctor told me if I was careful I could be moved, which my friends did, taking me to two miles east of Sulphur Springs. There the doctor visited me for several days, when it was again thought best to move me to Old Sumpter to Dr. Teagarden's. His son Billy, with whom I had been raised, was now with me. We got a hack and struck out for Sumpter, about twenty miles away. We started one night and got there before day. I received good treatment there and got along well, although I could not yet stand up well.

Everybody there tried to help me and everybody was my friend, but the infamous police were after me and there were several mischief-makers meddling about me. My friends again thought best to move me out two miles to John Gates', where I did not stay long. I came back again to Dr. Teagarden's. About the 27th of August I again had to leave the doctor's house, and that in a hurry, too.

They brought my horse up to the back gate and got me on him. By this time I had so improved that I could walk from the house to the yard, but was very weak and sore and could not straighten up. In company with Billy Teagarden and Charley we eluded a posse of police and went over into Angelina County, where we had an old friend by the name of Dave Harrel. We got there about the last of August, 1872. The Teagardens returned to Sumter.

After I had been at Harrel's for two days, word came that there was a party of police coming to arrest me. I got a double-barreled shotgun and resolved to sell my life dearly if they did come.

On or about the 1st of September two men rode up to the house, armed with Winchesters, and came in. They asked Mrs. Harrel if I was there, but she told them I was not. They cursed her for a damned liar and told her I was in the back room, but she denied them admittance.

I was in the back room all this time and heard all that was going on. I straightened myself up on my pallet, and as they darkened the door, I told them to hold up their hands; that they could not run over a woman and that I was going to protect that house. They turned around and left, saying they did not want to harm the woman, but were after John Wesley Hardin. They soon returned, but in the meantime I had sent for Dave Harrel, who was in the cotton patch near by, and he was saddling my horse to go to Till Watson's with me, about ten miles away.

The police by this time had opened the gate and were in the yard. Mrs. Harrel told them to get out of her yard and would not leave when we tried to get her to go to a neighbor's house.

These policemen came on with their Winchesters in their hands. I crawled to the back door and threw my shotgun to my shoulder as quickly as possible and fired, first at one, then at the other. In the meantime I had received a shot in my thigh, but Dave Harrel brought me my horse and helped me on him. We got to Till Watson's about dusk.

I learned afterwards that a coroner's inquest was held over one of the policemen and that the verdict was "that he had met death at the hands of an unknown party, from gunshot wounds."

I was now in a bad fix. I had a fresh wound which required immediate medical attention and my old wounds were giving me trouble again. I knew a mob were after me now, so I sent Dave Harrel to Rusk to tell the sheriff of Cherokee County, Dick Reagan, to come out and arrest me.

I told him to tell the sheriff that there was a reward for me and I would surrender to him rather than be made the victim of mob law. I told him to tell him to bring medical aid, but that for all this I wanted one-half the reward.

He brought four men with him, but kept them in the dark and made them believe he would have trouble in arresting me. They came to Till Watson's about the 4th of September, 1872. They came into the house, the deputies remaining on the gallery. The sheriff came in and said, "My name is Dick Reagan; I have come here to arrest you, as Dave Harrel told me you wished to surrender."

I told him yes, but a fair understanding made long friends. I told him I did not want to be put in jail; I wanted half the reward; I wanted medical aid; I wanted protection from mob law; I wanted to go to Austin as quickly as possible and from there to Gonzales.

He agreed to all this and said he would treat me right. He asked me where my arms were, and I told him one of my pistols was in the scabbard and the other under my head. I reached for it, and as I was pulling it out to give it to him, one of his men outside shot me on the right knee. I first thought on the impulse of the moment, that I would kill the sheriff, but it flashed across me at once that it was a mistake and that in him was my only protection. The sheriff and posse were all very sorry that this happened, and each man seemed to vie with each other in making me as comfortable as possible. They got a hack and put pillows and bed quilt in it trying to make my journey easy.

When we got to Rusk, they put me in a private home and sent for a doctor. They then took me to the hotel kept by Dick Reagan on the corner of the square. Thus I arrived at Rusk about the 7th of September, 1872, with four bullet holes in me.

Many different and varied kinds of people came to see me, some of them expecting to see a man with horns on his head and were surprised when they saw me, saying, "He looks just like we'uns." They would ask me all kinds of questions: how many men I had killed, if I had ever killed a woman, etc. Dr. Jimson soon got there and cleared out the room. They would come there day after day, however; some for curiosity and some for charity. I did my best to be polite to all callers.

Sheriff Reagan sent his son Dood to nurse me, and he and I soon became chums. Mrs. Reagan was also very kind to me and seemed to never tire of fixing me dainty dishes to tempt a sick man's appetite.

I kept thinking of my wife in Gonzales, but never mentioned her name. I would ask the doctor every day when I could be moved. I knew I was charged with several capital crimes in Gonzales, but believed I could come clear if I had a fair trial there.

In putting down Negro rule there, I had made many friends and sympathizers and had made it a thing of the past for a Negro to hold an office in that county.

Dick Reagan told me that whenever the doctor said I could be moved he would take me to Austin. We started for Austin on the 22nd of September, Deputy John Taylor going with the sheriff and I. On reaching Austin, we stopped at an hotel, and the next day they put me in an old jail down by the river. Barnhart Zimpelman was then sheriff there. Sheriff Reagan then went back to Rusk, and I waited for him some time to come back with my horse Joe and $450 in gold, for which I gave him an order on Till Watson. After waiting for his return several days, I concluded to see a lawyer, who got out a writ of habeas corpus, and I was ordered to be carried to Gonzales.

We had a code of laws of our own in that Austin jail, in which there were always about twenty-five jail birds. Whenever a new prisoner was brought in, we would all cry, "Fresh fish," and kangaroo court proceedings at once commenced. It was rarely the victim escaped without a fine or "shake." We would shake the "fresh fish" by getting hold of the corner of a blanket and tossing them nearly to the ceiling and then letting them fall.

While in that jail I got acquainted with Burns and Kimble, who were afterwards hung for the murder of a peddlar.

Some friends in Austin, knowing I was wounded, frequently sent me meals from the hotels, and I would always divide with my fellow prisoners. One of the prisoners, an overbearing devil, one day said I was stingy about dividing up, and made a grab for some custard I was eating. I let drive at him with my boot, which was iron heeled, and sent him sprawling and bleeding to the floor. The jailer got mad about it and said he would put the man that did it in irons. I told him I was that man and explained the circumstances. He didn't iron me.

In a day or two four State Policemen started with me to Gonzales, and when we got to Lockhart, they tried to make me ride a mule, as my horse was played out. My wounds were still painful and I did not like the looks of that mule. So one of the guards said he would let me ride his horse and he would ride that mule. Then a regular circus commenced, and the mule threw the policeman so high and hard that everybody made fun of him. He soon traded it off for a horse.

When we reached Gonzales, they had me shackled and chained to a horse, and the people there denounced such brutal treatment, saying that I had done more for the peace and welfare of the country than any other man in it.

Capt. Williams told the guards that they had just as well turn me loose as to leave me in Gonzales, but they put me in jail, where a blacksmith soon came and cut my irons off.

W. E. Jones was sheriff of Gonzales County then and told me that my friends would soon be in to see me and to keep quiet and patient.

As well as I can recollect, on or about the 10th of October, 1872, I cut into open daylight with a big saw, cutting through the iron bars on the south side. The guards on duty posted me when to work, as the saw made a big fuss. I got through late in the evening and waited until dark to leave the jail.

Manning Clements and Bud McFadden were there to see that I got off all right, and I rode Benny Anderson's iron gray horse home.

[Here follows a diversion from the story, and Hardin goes into a description of the political campaign of 1894 in Gonzales County. Feeling between Hardin and W. E. Jones ran high then, Jones being a candidate for sheriff. Hardin was supporting Coleman for sheriff against Jones, and brought up his escape from jail in 1872, when Jones was sheriff. He accused him (Jones) of knowing all about his cutting out and escape. This, as detailed above, Sheriff Jones strenuously denied. The manuscript quotes the letters from Jones and Hardin to the people of Gonzales verbatim, and not considering them germane to the subject treated, we have not published them.—Publishers.]

When I got home, I met my darling and beloved wife. My neighbors and friends all came to see me and congratulate me on my safe return. I stayed at home and recuperated until January, 1873, when I began driving cattle to Indianola and shipping to New Orleans. Cuero was our nearest railroad, being 25 miles off, and about the 9th of April, 1873, I started there on some business connected with the shipping of cattle and to match a race with a certain party if I could do so. Just as I was about to start, John Gay came to Manning Clements' house, where I happened to be, and told me they were opening a new road from Cuero to San Antonio by way of Rancho. The road came by Manning Clements', and Gay told me if I would follow his furrow across the prairie, I would save time and get to Cuero without any trouble. I got about 18 miles from home, opposite the Mustang mot, when I saw a man riding a gray horse off to the right of the road about 200 yards therefrom. I saw he was armed with a Winchester and that he had two six-shooters on the horn of his saddle. He turned a little to the right, apparently looking for cattle, I suppose to put me off my guard, but it really put me on my guard. I checked up, and he got down off his horse. I was now in the furrow leading to Cuero. I got down also, apparently to fix my saddle, but really to give him no advantage over me, for his arms and general appearance gave me the impression that he was either on the dodge or was an officer. He then mounted his horse and I did likewise, so we met face to face. We both stopped our horses, and he said, "Do you live around here?"

I told him I was traveling from San Antonio on my way to Cuero and "am trying to follow this furrow, which I am told will take me to Cuero." I asked him how far it was, and he said about seven miles. Then he remarked that he had been over to Jim Cox's to serve some papers on him. "I'm sheriff of this county," said he. I had understood up to this time that Dick Hudson was the acting sheriff of DeWitt. I said, "I suppose your name is Dick Hudson?"

He said no, but that Dick Hudson was his deputy and his name was Jack Helms.

I told him that my name was John Wesley Hardin. He says, "Are you Wesley?" at the same time offering me his hand.

I refused to take his hand and told him that he now had a chance to take me to Austin.

"We are man to man and face to face; on equal terms. You have said I was a murderer and a coward, and have had your deputies after me. Now arrest me if you can. I dare you to try it."

78

"Oh," he said, "Wesley, I am your friend, and my deputies are hunting you on their own account, and not mine."

I had drawn my pistol by this time, and he begged me to put it up and not to kill him. I said, "You are armed, defend yourself. You have been going round killing men long enough, and I know you belong to a legalized band of murdering cowards and have hung and murdered better men than yourself."

He said, "Wesley, I won't fight you, and I know you are too brave a man to shoot me. I have the governor's proclamation offering $500 for your arrest in my pocket, but I will never try to execute it if you will spare my life; I will be your friend."

I told him his deputies were putting themselves to a lot of trouble about me and that I would hold him responsible for their actions. Well, I let him alone and we rode on together to Cuero. We separated about two miles from Cuero, agreeing to meet next day in town and come to an understanding.

Well, we met as agreed, and he wanted me to join his vigilant company, of which he was captain. I declined, because the people with whom he was waging war were my friends. I told him all I asked of him was that I and my immediate friends should be neutral. This was understood, and we parted, agreeing to meet again on the 16th, he bringing one of his party, and I bringing Manning Clements and George Tennille.

I remained in town, finished my business, and went to a bar room on the southwest corner of the square. I took a drink with some friends and then went into a back room where a poker game was going on and joined the play. It was a freeze out for $5 and I won the pot. We all went to the bar, and a man named J. B. Morgan rushed up to me and wanted me to treat him to a bottle of champagne. I declined to do this. He got furious and wanted to fight, starting to draw a pistol on me. Some friends of mine caught him, and I walked out, saying that I wished no row. I walked outside and was talking to a friend. I had forgotten all about Morgan when he came up again; told me I had insulted him and had to fight. He asked me if I was armed. I told him I was. He pulled his pistol halfway out, remarking, "Well, it is time you were defending yourself."

I pulled my pistol and fired, the ball striking him just above the left eye. He fell dead. I went to the stable, got my horse, and left town unmolested.

The coroner held an inquest over his dead body, but what the inquest was I never learned. Afterward (about four years) I heard I was indicted for the murder of J. B. Morgan, and about seven years afterward I entered a plea of guilty to the charge of manslaughter, getting two years in the penitentiary for it.

In the year 1873, and in fact previous to this date, there existed in Gonzales and DeWitt counties a vigilant committee that made life, liberty, and property uncertain. This vigilant band was headed by Jack Helms, the sheriff of DeWitt, and his most able lieutenants were his deputies, Jim Cox, Joe Tomlinson, and Bill Sutton. Some of the best men in the country had been murdered by this mob. Pipkin Taylor had been decoyed by them at night from his house and shot down because he did not indorse the killing of his own sons-in-law, Henry and Will Kelly, by this brutal Helms' mob. Anyone who did not indorse their foul deeds or go with them on their raids incurred their hatred, and it meant death at their hands. They were about 200 strong at this time and were waging a war with the Taylors and their friends.

About the 1st of April, Jim Taylor shot Bill Sutton seriously in Cuero one night in a billiard hall. Such was the state of affairs when Manning Clements, George Tennille, and myself went to Jim Cox's house to meet Jack Helms and Jim Cox, the acknowledged leaders of the vigilant band. When we got there, they took me off and said they could and would work me out of all trouble if I would but join them. They said there were but two sides—for them or against them. I talked as if I would join them, and they told me of a dozen or more of my friends whom they wished to kill, and who were the best men in the community, their sin lying in the fact that they did not endorse the vigilant committee's murdering. They told me they would have to do a whole lot of work to get me clear of all trouble, so I would have to do a whole lot for them, and they went so far as to say that if George Tennille and Manning Clements did not join them, they would have to be killed. I told them then that neither George Tennille, Manning Clements, nor myself would join them; that we wanted peace. I told them that I would not swap work with them, but that they and their mob must keep out of our country and let us alone. They agreed to this and said that they would let me know if any danger threatened me, but swore eternal vengeance on the Taylors and their friends.

When they had gone, I told Manning and George just what had passed between us, and George remarked that it would not be a week before the murdering cowards made a raid on us.

About the 23rd of April, 1873, Jack Helms and fifty men came into our neighborhood and inquired for Manning, George, and myself. They insulted the women folks and Jack Helms was particularly insulting to my wife because she would not inform him of some of the Taylor party. We were all out hunting cattle at the time, and when we came back and found out what had happened, we determined to stop this way of doing, and sent word to the Taylors to meet us at the Mustang mot in order to concot a plan of campaign.

There I met Jim, John, and Scrap Taylor, while Manning Clements, George Tennille, and myself represented our side of the house. It was there agreed to fight mob law to the bitter end, as our lives and families were in danger.

A fight came off not long afterwards near Tomlinson Creek, in which Jim Cox, one of the leaders of the vigilant committee, and Jake Christman were killed. It was currently reported that I led the fight, but as I have never pleaded to that case, I will at this time have little to say, except to state hat Jim Cox and Jake Chrisman met their death from the Taylor party about the 15th of May, 1873.

On the 17th I was to meet Jack Helms at a little town called Albukirk in Wilson County. I went there according to agreement, a trusty friend accompanying me in the person of Jim Taylor. We talked matters over together and failed to agree, he seriously threatening Jim Taylor's life, and so I went and told Jim to look out, that Jack Helms had sworn to shoot him on sight because he had shot Bill Sutton and because he was a Taylor. Jim quickly asked me to introduce him to Helms or point him out. I declined to do this, but referred him to a friend that would. I went to a blacksmith shop and had my horse shod. I paid for the shoeing and was fixing to leave when I heard Helms' voice: "Hands up, you d—— s—— of a b——."

I looked around and saw Jack Helms advancing on Jim Taylor with a large knife in his hands. Some one hollered, "Shoot the d——d scoundrel." It appeared to me that Helms was the scoundrel, so I grabbed my shotgun and

THE KILLING OF JACK HELMS

fired at Capt. Jack Helms as he was closing with Jim Taylor. I then threw my gun on the Helms crowd and told them not to draw a gun, and made one fellow put up his pistol. In the meantime Jim Taylor had shot Helms repeatedly in the head, so thus did the leader of the vigilant committee, the sheriff of DeWitt, the terror of the country, whose name was a horror to all law-abiding citizens, meet his death. He fell with twelve buckshot in his breast and several six-shooter balls in his head. All of this happened in the midst of his own friends and advisors, who stood by utterly amazed. The news soon spread that I had killed Jack Helms and I received many letters of thanks from the widows of the men whom he had cruelly put to death. Many of the best citizens of Gonzales and DeWitt counties patted me on the back and told me that was the best act of my life.

On the 18th of May, 1873, we got news of a mob of fifty men under the leadership of Joe Tomlinson who were coming into our neighborhood to kill and raid us in revenge. We concluded at once to go and meet them, and thirteen of us got together. It was about fifteen miles to where they were making their headquarters at Joe Tomlinson's place, four miles west of Yorktown. We found out that there were about fifty men in and around the house and that at night most of them slept on the galleries. We got there at 2 A.M. in the night of the 18th and agreed that we should slip up to the gallery, and if we did this undiscovered, to fire upon the sleeping mob. But the vigilants' dogs soon announced our arrival and that game was up. We then sent runners to our friends for more help, detailing three men to do this. The remaining ten were to hold the enemy in the house until reinforcements came, when we would clean them out. Our forces began arriving about 4 P.M., and we were fixing to attack them when a party led by Deputy Sheriff Dave

Blair made its appearance to relieve the Tomlinson party in the house. I took five men and headed them off in front of the house, and, in fact, captured Blair right in front of his friends. When he declared that he was there to relieve Tomlinson, I told him that was just what I was there to prevent and he had just as well commence work on me.

"Well," he said, "under the circumstances I won't persist, especially as all my men have deserted me."

Things began to get in shape for a good fight when some of the best citizens of the county came out to where we were preparing for battle. We had about seventy-five men and they had fifty. These men were the means of preventing a collision, and through their efforts a treaty was made which each and every one of both parties should sign. It was agreed that we should go to Clinton, the county seat of DeWitt County, and have this arrangement recorded, which we did the following day, the 20th of May, 1873.

I resumed work again and commenced to ship and drive cattle without anything tragical happening until December, 27th, 1873, when Wiley Prigon was attacked by four men and murdered in his store eight miles below Cuero. Prigon was a Taylor man and his murderers belonged to the Sutton gang. Thus was war stirred up between the two parties again.

They met this time at Cuero, each party trying to get the drop on the other. Shooting was the order of the day, but finally friends of both parties undertook to pacify them and an armistice was agreed to, both parties again signing articles of peace.

My wife and baby had taken a trip to Comanche to see my parents and my brother Joe's family.

On the 1st of January, 1874, leaving my cattle business in my father-in-law's hands, I pulled out for Comanche. Dr.

J. Brosius went with me. At Austin I got sick, and we continued our journey in a buggy. I met my wife and baby, Molly, in Comanche with my parents and brothers and sisters. I stayed there until the latter part of January and then, in company with my wife and baby, Dr. Brosius, and Gip Clements, started home for Gonzales County by way of San Saba and Llano.

While in Comanche I had bought a race horse named "Rondo," and I carried him with me on my way to Gonzales. I stopped at Llano and while there bought a herd of steers for the market and made a race for $500, which I easily won. So I journeyed on to Gonzales and reached home about the 15th of February. I then began gathering cattle for Kansas.

In the meantime the Sutton party had violated their pledges and on several occasions had turned our cattle loose.

In April, 1874, Sutton started some cattle north, and he himself was going by rail to Wichita, Kansas. We had often tried to catch him, but he was so wily that he always eluded us. Jim Taylor had shot him and broken his arm in a saloon in Cuero. He had a horse killed under him in a fight on the prairie below Cuero and he had another killed while crossing the river below there. He was looked upon as hard to catch, and I had made futile efforts to get him myself. I had even gone down to his home at Victoria, but did not get him.

In March my brother Joe and Aleck Barrickman came down from Comanche to visit me, and after he had stayed several days, I got him to go to Indianola, our shipping point. I told Joe that Bill Sutton was my deadly enemy and that he was soon going to Kansas by way of New Orleans.

I told him to find out when Sutton would leave Indianola so that I could tell Jim Taylor and go at once to Indianola to kill him, as it was a life or death case whenever either I or Jim Taylor met him. So my brother and Barrickman went down there and attended to my shipping interests and in doing so got acquainted with Bill Sutton and found out when he would leave Indianola on the steamer "Clinton." He let me know at once and I told Jim Taylor. Jim took Billy Taylor with him and went to Indianola. They went to my brother, who was boarding at Pat Smith's, who kept them informed as to when Sutton and party would board the "Clinton." In the meantime he had hired two of the best horses in town for them to leave on. Besides that, there were six or eight brave men ready there who stood in with the play. The plan was to let Sutton and his crowd go aboard and then for Jim and Billy Taylor to follow and commence shooting as soon as they saw him. Bill Sutton, his wife, and Gabe Slaughter passed in at one of the dining hall doors. Jim and Billy Taylor met them and immediately began shooting. Sutton tried to draw his pistol, but failed, being pierced through the head and heart with Jim Taylor's bullets. Meanwhile a deadly fight was going on between Billy Taylor and Gabe Slaughter. Gabe Slaughter had found out that Jim Taylor was going to shoot Sutton and called out, "Look out, Billy," when Billy Taylor turned round on him, saying, "Look out yourself, you d—— s—— of a b——."

He fired on Gabe Slaughter, who was drawing his pistol, and Slaughter fell with Sutton, a pistol in his hand and a bullet in his head.

The Taylor boys passed out of the "Clinton" on to the wharf and came up to the stock pens where my hands were branding cattle. There they got horses and came at once to Cuero, about sixty miles from Indianola, and from thence up to where I was branding cattle for the trail.

It was now April, and I soon started my cattle for Wichita, Kansas, and put Joe Clements in charge. I was to receive the cattle in June at or near Wichita, but was not going with the cattle myself.

About this time my brother Joe and my cousin, Aleck Barrickman, went home to Comanche, and my wife and baby went with them to visit my parents there. It was understood that I should spend a week with them on my way up to Kansas.

Jim Taylor and I agreed to start another herd, as Ed Glover, Jim, Joe, Gip, and Manning were all going up the trail, he (Jim) did not want to be left in that country by himself. In about two weeks we had complied with the laws and had started another herd of about 1,000 head. We placed Dr. J. B. Brosius in charge with instructions to go by Hamilton, in Hamilton County, and they were there to send me word at Comanche, where I would be with my parents.

About the 23rd of April, 1874, Jim Taylor and I left Gonzales, bound first for Comanche and then for Wichita.

In the meantime Rube Brown had arrested Billy Taylor and had sent him at once to Galveston, so we never had a chance to rescue him. There was also a reward of $500 offered for Jim Taylor.

We got to Comanche on or about the 28th of April, having Rondo and two other race horses with us. It was not long before I made two races to be run on the Comanche tracks on the 26th of May, 1874. I was to run Rondo against a mare that had beaten him before. My brother had a horse named "Shiloh" which I also matched, and a cousin of mine, Bud Dixon, matched a horse of his called "Dock."

The 26th of May was my birth day. About the 5th, Jim Taylor and I went with my brother and the sheriff's party some twenty miles into Brown County to get some cattle that belonged to my brother. The cattle were in possession of the Gouldstones, and we got them and started back without any trouble. Night overtaking us, we stopped at Mrs. Waldrup's to pen our cattle. At the supper table Mrs. Waldrup told us how one Charles Webb, a deputy sheriff of Brown County, had come to her house and arrested Jim Buck Waldrup and had cursed and abused her. She had told him that no gentleman would curse a woman. Of course, we all agreed with her. This is the first time I had ever heard of Charles Webb. There were present that night at the supper table Bill Cunningham, Bud and Tom Dixon, Jim and Ham Anderson, Aleck Barrickman, Jim Taylor and Jim Milligan (deputy sheriffs), Joe Hardin, Jim Taylor [sic], and myself. We were all first cousins to each other except Jim Taylor. There is no doubt but that we all sympathized with Mrs. Waldrup, who had been so abused by Charles Webb. On my trial afterwards for the killing of Webb the State relied on a conspiracy being formed at the supper table to kill Webb, and they used Cunningham to prove it, but they utterly failed, or else they would have broken my neck or found me guilty of murder in the first degree. The evidence that Cunningham gave on my trial was that my brother Joe (who was not indicted with me) had said, "We will get away with him at the proper time." That statement was an absolute lie. Cunningham was supposed to be our friend, but at my trial was looked upon as one of my brother's murderers and my enemy. But to return to my story.

We drove the cattle home next morning to Comanche,

and from that until the 26th but one more incident worthy of note occurred.

Henry Ware was a bully from Canada, and from some cause or other he disliked my brother Joe. He came to the herd one day (Jim Taylor told me this) and claimed a cow, and my brother told him he could not get it. Ware persisted and put his hand to his Winchester, when my brother ordered him out of the herd at the point of a six-shooter, an order which the Hon. Henry Ware promptly obeyed, and he did not get his cow.

The 26th of May saw a big crowd at the races, the news of which had been published all over the country. Rondo ran first and won easily. Shiloh came next and had a walk over. Next came Dock, which was a close race, but he won by six feet. So I and my friends won everything in sight. I won about $3,000 in cash, fifty head of cattle, a wagon or two, and fifteen head of saddle horses. I set more than one man afoot and then loaned them the horses to ride home on.

I had heard that morning that Charles Webb, the deputy sheriff from Brown County, had come over to Comanche with fifteen men to kill me and capture Jim Taylor for the reward. I also heard that he had said that John Carnes, the sheriff of Comanche, was no man or sheriff because he allowed a set of murderers to stay around him, headed by the notorious John Wesley Hardin, and as he (Carnes) would not attend to his business, he would do it for him. I knew that Webb had arrested a whole cow camp a short time before and had treated a man whom he called John Wesley Hardin most cruelly, telling him he was afraid of his own name and jabbed him in the side with his gun, knowing positively that I was not in the country at that time. If I had been there, I would have taught him a lesson sooner.

He did not make any breaks at the race tracks, but when we all came back to town, he swore time and time again that he would kill me and capture Jim Taylor, and that this would be done before the sun went down. When I was told this, I laughed and said I hoped he would put it off till dark or altogether.

We were all going from bar to bar, trying to spend some of the money we had won. I remember in one saloon I threw a handful of $20 gold pieces on the counter and called for the drinks. Some of my friends picked them up and thought I was drinking too freely, and told me if any scrap came up, I would not be able to protect myself. I assured them I was all right, but at last thought I had better go home to avoid any possible trouble.

I got Jeff Hardin, my little brother, to go to my brother Joe's stable and get his horse and buggy to drive out to my father's, who lived about two miles northwest from town. I bought such supplies as were needed at home and told Jeff to put them in the buggy and then to come up to Jack Wright's saloon on the corner, where Jim Taylor and myself would drive out to my father's.

We invited the whole crowd up to Jack Wright's to take a last drink. Frank Wilson, a deputy sheriff under Carnes, came up and locked arms with me just as I was going to drink and said, "John, I want to see you."

I said all right.

This saloon was situated on the northwest corner of the square, the front facing the square to the east, with a door in front, and another door to the north near the west end of the saloon. Frank Wilson and I went out at the north door and then west for about ten steps, when I told him that was far enough and stopped on the back street west of the saloon. Frank said, "John, the people here have treated you well; now don't drink any more, but go home and avoid all trouble."

I told him Jeff had gone for the buggy, and I was going as soon as he came. He said, "You know it is a violation of the law to carry a pistol."

I knew now that he was trying to pump me, so I told him my pistol was behind the bar and threw open my coat to show him. But he did not know I had a good one under my vest. I looked to the south and saw a man, a stranger to me, with two six-shooters on coming towards us. I said to Frank, "Let's go back to the saloon. I want to pay my bill and then go home."

We went into the saloon and we were stopped by Jim Taylor, who said, "Wes, you have drank enough; let us go home; here is Jeff with the buggy."

I said, "Let us go in and get a cigar, then we will go home."

About this time Dave Carnes remarked, "Here comes that damned Brown County sheriff."

I turned around and faced the man whom I had seen coming up the street. He had on two six-shooters and was about fifteen steps from me, advancing. He stopped when he got to within five steps of me, then stopped and scrutinized me closely, with his hands behind him. I asked him, "Have you any papers for my arrest?"

He said, "I don't know you."

I said, "My name is John Wesley Hardin."

He said, "Now I know you, but have no papers for your arrest."

"Well," I said, "I have been informed that the sheriff of Brown County has said that Sheriff Carnes of this county was no sheriff or he would not allow me to stay around Comanche with my murdering pals."

92

He said, "I am not responsible for what the sheriff of Brown County says. I am only a deputy."

So Dave Carnes spoke up and said, "Men, there can be no difference between you about John Carnes," and said, "Mr. Webb, let me introduce you to Mr. Hardin."

I asked him what he had in his hand behind his back, and he showed me a cigar. I said, "Mr. Webb, we were just going to take a drink or a cigar; won't you join us?"

He replied, "Certainly." As I turned around to go in the north door, I heard some one say, "Look out, Jack." It was Bud Dixon, and as I turned around, I saw Charles Webb drawing his pistol. He was in the act of presenting it when I jumped to one side, drew my pistol, and fired.

In the meantime, Webb had fired, hitting me in the left side, cutting the length of it, inflicting an ugly and painful wound. My aim was good and a bullet hole in the left cheek did the work. He fell against the wall, and as he fell he fired a second shot, which went into the air.

In the meantime, my friends, Jim Taylor and Bud Dixon, seeing that Webb had taken the drop on me and had shot me, pulled their pistols and fired on him as he was falling, not knowing that I had killed him. Each shot hit him in the side and breast.

At my first attempt to shoot, Frank Wilson started to draw his pistol, but as soon as I had fired on Webb and before Wilson had time to draw, I covered him and told him to hold up his hands, which he did.

Several men were standing at the east end of the building next to the public square. When the shooting commenced, they started to rush over to the saloon, but soon retreated.

I afterwards learned the plan was for Charles Webb to assassinate me and then for the crowd to rush up and with

Frank Wilson's help to rush in and overpower Jim Taylor, thus getting the reward. They expected my relatives and friends to stand still while they did their bloody work. They believed they could not arrest Taylor without killing me, hence they attacked me.

The crowd outside ran back, as I stated above, and cried out, "Hardin has killed Charley Webb; let us hang him."

The sheriff of the county, John Carnes, who was my friend, came in with a shot gun and asked, "Who did this work?"

I told him I had done it, and would surrender to him if he would protect me from the mob. I handed him my pistol to show my good faith.

About ten men ran around the east corner and commenced firing on us and Jim Taylor. Bud Dixon and Aleck Barrickman drew their pistols and started to fire, when they ran back behind the corner. They were reinforced and charged again, John Carnes met them at the door and demanded that they disperse. They overpowered and disarmed him of his gun and were trying to get my pistol away from him. I told my friends that there was no protection for us there, and told Jim Taylor to come with me and the other two to go back west. So Jim and I ran across the street to some horses that were hitched near by, and as I ran I pulled my knife out of my pocket and cut the hitching ropes.

I now saw that my wife and sister Mat were in the crowd crying and looking down towards my brother's law office. I saw my father and brother Joe coming toward the scene with shotguns.

I concluded the best thing to do to avoid bloodshed was to get out of town. Jim Taylor wanted to charge the mob, but I said, "For God's sake, don't do that; you may hit the wrong one." (He told me afterwards he wanted to kill Henry Ware.) I caught his horse and kept him from shooting. We turned and went running out of town, the mob firing on us and the sheriff's party trying to protect us.

Dixon and Anderson, seeing we were safely out of town, got on their horses also, and we met again at my father's, where my father and brother joined us with the sheriff.

I was willing to surrender, but the sheriff said he could not protect me; that the mob was too strong, and Charley Webb had been their leader. He advised me to stay around until the excitement died down and then come in and surrender.

So I went to some mountains about four miles off, and next day my brother and some friends came out to see me and my party, and by them I sent back the horses we had gotten out of town on and two pistols we had found in the saddle pockets.

At that time there were some companies of Rangers there who were organized to keep the peace and protect the frontier from Indians. They took the place of the infamous State Police. Bill Waller was their captain, and he wished to make himself famous at once. The sheriff told him he could and would arrest me whenever he was sure he could protect me. He tried to get Waller to assist him in doing this, but Waller was really the captain of a "vigilant" band and would not do it. Even my father and brother told Waller that if he would himself guarantee me protection, I would come in and surrender. Waller could guarantee nothing, but persisted in hunting me with his mob, composed of the enemies of all law and order. He aroused the whole country and had about 500 men scouting for me, whose avowed purpose was to hang me. Waller arrested my father and Barrickman's family and took them to Comanche to my brother's, where he put them under guard under the pretense of keeping them from giving me any information. They then arrested my brother, with Tom and Bud Dixon, and placed them in the courthouse under guard. They also arrested Dr. Brosius, who had come to tell us that our herd was at Hamilton. In fact, there were squads of from 50 to 100 in each party hunting for me all over the country, and instead of the excitement dying out, it grew greater all the time. Once, two scouting parties met and fired upon each other, keeping it up for two hours until each drew off for reinforcements.

They had now cut me off from all communication with my relatives and friends and were "brushing" the country for me.

About the night of the 1st of June, 1874, we camped about six miles west of Comanche in a valley close to a creek that had a large pool of water in it about two miles below. Water was very scarce and we got most of our water from this pool. The Rangers found it out, and we had several fights at or near the spring. On this night they found two of our horses. Jim Taylor, Aleck Barrickman, Ham Anderson, and myself stayed together at night, but scouted in the daytime, and I could not impress on Barrickman and Anderson the gravity of the situation. They could not understand how the feeling could be so bitter against us, and they knew how well my father stood and that my brother Joe had a host of friends. They kept saying that there was no danger, and I could not even get them to stake their horses at night.

On the night of the 1st of January [*sic*], about 100 men in a party found their horses not far off. They caught the horses and camped on a hill in a clump of live oaks about

600 yards from where we were down in the valley. About 2 o'clock I got up and re-staked Frank and Dock, mine and Jim's horses, and as I could not see the other horses, I woke up Ham and Aleck and told them their horses were gone. They got up to hunt them and soon came back reporting the presence of the scouters and saying that there must be at least 150 of them. I thought they were waiting till day to attack, so I concluded to move camp at once. The moon was shining brightly when we pulled out. Two men were on foot, packing their saddles simply because they were fools enough not to stake their horses when their lives were at stake. I told Ham and Aleck to go to a spot near a spring and we would go and get some horses from a place near there where Joe had some saddle horses running loose. So we parted, Jim Taylor and I going after the horses, Ham and Aleck going down the creek, their saddles and blankets on their back. It was not long before we found the bunch of saddle horses, drove them to the pen and caught the two best.

We started back for the boys when I saw a man coming towards the pen. We saw he was lost. He got within ten steps of me when I threw my shotgun down on him and told him his life depended on his actions. The moon was shining brightly and Jim Taylor had caught his bridle. He said, "John, for God's sake don't kill me."

I asked him who he was and he said, "I am your friend, but I am a Ranger. We found your horses tonight and knew you were close by. They sent me to Comanche for reinforcements. By daylight you will have 300 men around you and escape will be impossible. If they catch you, they are going to hang you."

I then said to Jim, "We had better kill him; dead men tell no tales."

He said, "Oh, for God's sake, don't kill me; I'll never tell on you and will do anything for you."

After satisfying myself that he would do to trust, I gave him a $20 gold piece to give to my wife and told him to tell her to go to Gonzales, where I was going to start for next morning. I told her not to be uneasy about me; that I would never surrender alive and that Jim and I had agreed to die together. That if either of our horses were shot down, we would take the other up, but that we expected to be run up on before we got out of the country.

After many pledges of fidelity on his part we let him go and took the horses to our companions. When we got there, I told them that Jim and I were going to leave the country, and if they wanted to go with us to say so quickly. They wanted us to stay and go to Bill Stones' house, a man whom they had lately helped out of trouble and whom they looked on as a friend. They said they had done nothing and no one would hurt them. So they said they would stay and go to Bill Stones'. I told them to leave the country as Jim and I were going to do; that they did not have to go with us, but to go anywhere, so that they got away from this country. I told them that Bill Stones would betray them if they went there; that these were no times to trust such men. They still said they were going, so I pulled out five $20 gold pieces and told them to divide it among them, and so we bade them good-bye. It proved to be a last farewell. They went to Stones', who betrayed them, and they were shot to death.

It was now daylight and Jim and I had to go out on the prairie to go the way we wanted to. To our right where we had camped, the valley was full of men, so we turned to the left. The country was very rough and rugged, deep gulches making it almost impassable except at certain places.

The Rangers by this time had spied us and were after us, but as we were a quarter of a mile ahead, we felt perfectly safe. We went on, crossing gulch after gulch, until we crossed a very deep one just before coming to the Brownwood and Comanche road. There was a long hill on the other side, and just as we got to the summit, we ran right upon Capt. Waller himself and 200 men. These were the reinforcements going out to meet the other Rangers, who were now pursuing us. Capt. Waller ordered his men to halt and told us to surrender. I said, "Jim, look out! Follow me!" Putting spurs to Frank, I went down the mountain, with Capt. Waller, his men, and the bullets flying behind us.

Seeing that we must now meet our former pursuers, who were crossing the gulch at the only crossing, I said, "Jim, let us charge them and double them up as quick as lightning." So we wheeled again, and Jim being ahead, I told him to hold Dock, as he was a fast quarter horse and my Frank was a mile horse. We were now charging up hill right among Waller's men, who were afraid to fire for fear of hitting each other. Often in the charge I would tell a man to drop his gun and he would obey me. Jim fired several shots, and as we were passing out of the lines, I saw a man aiming at him. I told him to drop his gun, which he did. We had passed out of the lines when some one upbraided him for his cowardice and he picked it up again and fired at us, hitting Frank in the hind leg but not hurting him enough to make him lame.

It was now about 9 A.M. and drizzling rain. Capt. Waller apparently conceived the idea of running on us and turned his horse loose after us for that purpose. I told Jim to hold up as I wanted to kill him. I wheeled, stopped my horse, and cocked my shotgun. I had a handkerchief over the tubes to keep the caps dry, and just as I pulled the trigger, the wind blew it back and the hammer fell on the handkerchief. That saved his life. Waller checked up his horse and broke back to his men.

Jim and I went on about 200 yards further and got down to see what the damage was. We found that Frank was shot, as were also our saddles and clothes, but that we were unhurt. The pursuing party fixing to surround us again, we got on our horses again and ran off from them. It seemed to me as if their horses stood still. We were riding race horses. I had refused $500 for Frank and $250 for Dock. Good horseflesh is a good thing in a tight.

After running off from our pursuers, we thought ourselves pretty safe, as they were behind us and we were riding good horses. In this, however, we were mistaken, for we presently came up on twenty-five men who were hunting us, but we got around them all right. We went boldly on, going around the town of Comanche and striking the Hamilton and Comanche road ten or twelve miles further on. It was raining hard and the country, as well as being rough, was covered with water, making the roads almost impassable. We thought we had done well, considering all this, to say nothing of the scouting parties we had to avoid.

We went on to Bud Tatum's, just eighteen miles from Comanche, and we "hollered" and asked if we could stay all night. He told us to get down, and I laid my double-barreled shotgun down alongside the fence, as I did not want to appear too heavily armed. After we had put up our horses and eaten supper, I told the old man that we wanted an early start in the morning. He did not recognize us and promised to get us off early in the morning. He woke us up an hour before day and told us he had fed our horses. At the breakfast table he recognized me and asked me why I did not make myself known to him last night. I told him

I did not want to alarm him. I was tired and did not want to take chances on his going and reporting on me. He told us good-bye and said, "Don't be afraid of this old man. I am a friend of your father and brother Joe."

I got him to fix us up grub enough for a three days' tramp for two men. I told him to go out to the gate, get my double-barreled gun and give it to my brother next time he went to town. He told me he was going that way, so I pulled out five $20 gold pieces and told him to give them to my wife.

Thus we stopped on the public road eighteen miles from Comanche that first night. Thirty rangers had passed by, going to Hamilton County to arrest the hands around our herd, but they never knew that we were at old Bud Tatum's. They had actually taken my brother's saddle horse, his race horse, and my wife's buggy horses and mounted them to help hunt us. Jim and I, however, did not propose to be caught like rats and made our way to Austin, arriving at Fancy Jim Taylor's on the night of the 5th of June.

He lived six miles northwest of Austin in the cedar brakes, and we concluded to stay there and rest awhile.

On the night of the 17th, my cook, with Charley and Alf Day, rode up and told us that thirty Rangers had come out to the herd in Hamilton County, arrested the hands, had taken charge of the cattle, and that they had barely escaped arrest. They had taken, they said, the rest of the hands to Comanche and held them there. On the 5th inst., they told me, the mob had hung my brother, Joe G. Hardin, Tom and Bud Dixon, my cousins, and had shot to death Ham Anderson and Aleck Barrickman on their pallets at Bill Stones'. Jim Taylor was sick and hardly able to ride, so we agreed to separate, as he wanted to go to Gonzales. Alf Day was his nephew and he went with him.

I went on the night of the 8th to the Colorado River with them and saw them safely through the city of Austin. I bade Jim Taylor good-bye there for the last time and divided my purse with him, giving him ten $20 gold pieces to help him along.

I went back to Fancy Jim's, changed horses and with a friend, Rodgers, started back for Comanche.

We rode mostly at night and rested during the day. We got to old Bud Tatum's about sundown on the 10th, and I sent Rodgers up to Bud's to inquire into the situation. Bud had just come from Comanche and was loaded with information. He confirmed the report of the hanging and killing of my kinfolks. He said that any stranger going to Comanche was liable to be arrested and hung. He said to Rodgers, "I would not go to town if I were you, but would go some other way unless you wish to be hung."

Now I was convinced that my brother and relatives had been foully murdered. Up to this time I could not even entertain the idea. I knew that up to the time I killed Webb, no living man stood higher in the estimation of his neighbors as a man or a lawyer than my brother Joe.

Nothing would do me now but to go to Comanche. My companion tried to dissuade me, but in vain. I told him we would go to father's that night, prowl around, and see what we could learn.

About 12 o'clock we got to father's house. We unhitched our horses and unsaddled them back of the field. We then fed them and proceeded cautiously to the house. The last time we had been there was on the 30th of May, when thirty men were guarding the house and had fired on us. Talk about hearing bullets hiss and sing! The air was full of them that night, and they whistled over my head as they had never done before.

On this occasion we went to the well and began drawing water. I saw a man coming towards the well and waited until he got about ten steps from me, when I leveled my Winchester and told him his life depended on his actions. He said, "For God's sake, John, don't shoot me. I am staying here on purpose to see you. Your father has me employed to do the work in the house and round the garden patch. Nobody suspects me. I gave your wife that $20 gold piece you gave me at the horse pen. They are well, but they have hung Joe, Bud, and Tom and killed Ham and Aleck."

I said, "Hello, Dick; is that you?"

He said: Yes."

"Let us shake hands," said I, and he came forward and proved to be the same Dick Wade whom Jim and I had arrested at the horse pens on the night of the 1st.

He then told me all about how the mob of 150 men had, on the night of the 5th, in the dead hours of midnight, come into the town of Comanche, had thrown ropes around the necks of Joe, Bud, and Tom, and had led them, bareheaded and barefooted, through the streets and out to some post oaks near by, where they hung them until they were dead. He said that the next day old Bill Stones had led another band to his ranch and had shot to death Ham Anderson and Aleck Barrickman while they were sleeping on their pallets at his house.

I asked him where they buried Joe, and he showed me where he lay buried near two live oaks. I stayed there by my brother's grave and sent Dick to town to see my father, but father would not let him awake my dear, sleeping wife, for he knew she would come to me, which meant death to me and all.

Father and Dick talked the matter over, but father

thought it imprudent for him to come and see me. He told Dick to tell me that Jane and Molly, with Barrickman's family, were guarded to keep them from giving any possible information. "Tell him," he said, "that if they find out he is in the country, they will kill me and wind up the family. Tell him not to surrender under any circumstances."

So Dick came back to my brother's grave at about 3 A.M. He told me all my father had said. Right there over my brother's grave I swore to avenge my brother's death, and could I but tell you what I have done in that way without laying myself liable, you would think I have kept my pledge well. While I write this, I say from the deepest depths of my heart that my desire for revenge is not satisfied, and if I live another year, I promise my friends and my God to make another of my brother's murderers bite the dust. Just as long as I can find one of them and know for certain that he participated in the murder of my brother, just that and nothing more, right there, be the consequences what they may, I propose to take life.

It was now about 4 A.M. and whatever I was going to do had to be done quickly. I concluded to leave the country at once and go to Gonzales. If it had not been for my father and the women and children, I would not have left, but Waller had said that if I was seen in the country, they would kill father and my little brother Jeff and wind up on the women and children. No one unless he had a heart as black and bloodthirsty as Bill Waller's could ever have made such a threat, or conceived such thoughts, so I woke my companion (from whom I had kept most of this news) and bidding Dick good-bye, we saddled our horses. I saddled Frank and he saddled a mule. I then told Rodgers just what was the matter; who I was and the extent of the danger. He said, "Good God! I had no idea that you were

104

John Wesley Hardin; all the money in the world would not have induced me knowingly to accompany you on such a trip, and here I am traveling to my grave with the notorious John Wesley Hardin at $2 a day."

I said, "You've got a pistol, haven't you?"

He said he had.

I asked him what he was going to do if a squad ran on us. He studied a while and said, "Well, I hired for the trip and will go through. I will use the pistol for my boss if necessary."

We pulled out of Comanche about daylight and struck out for Lampasas on a straight line, over mountains and hills, when about 10 A.M. a scouting party ran on us. The mule had gotten leg sore and could not strike a lope. I would stop and let the party come up to within 200 or 300 yards of us, send a bullet from a needle gun over their heads, while my companion rode slowly along. Then I would catch up with him and again use my needle gun. We kept this up until it became monotonous. We then concluded to ride on together and if they ran on us, would fight it out together. At last we struck a creek and there we left our pursuers. We forged ahead until nearly sundown, when we began to get into the neighborhood of Lampasas. We saw a farm ahead, and there we stopped, for Frank was almost as slow as the mule now. We rode up to the house to see if there were any horses hitched or staked which we could get. We saw an iron gray horse staked in the field, and we concluded to get him. The plan was for Rodgers to take Frank and the mule to Fancy Jim's near Austin and for me to go on. I went out to the field, caught the horse, and saddled him. I bid Rodgers good-bye and told him to take his time. I thought I had a good horse, but soon found out that I was wrong. It took me until nearly

105

daylight to get to a friend's house about eighteen miles off. When I got to his house at daylight, I found my nag had seen better days and was "stove up." I said to my friend, "I am in a tight and this horse is not mine. I want you to send it back to the owner and tell him to charge it to John Wesley Hardin. I want your sorrel stallion. What is he worth?"

The owner said he did not wish to sell him much, but would take $250 for him. Well, I told him to catch him quickly and offered him the money. He told me to give it to the old lady. So I counted out to her thirteen $20 gold pieces. She said, "John, I nursed you when you were a baby; take back this gold piece. I sympathize with you and want you never to stop killing those Comanche devils who hung Joe."

I told her I had plenty of money to do me and thanked her for her kindness.

By this time Mr. Nix had come with the sorrel horse, and when I started out to him, Mrs. Nix told me to wait for my breakfast, which I did.

While I was eating my breakfast Mrs. Nix went to my saddle pockets and put $250 in them, which I found afterwards.

In the meantime a squad of men came up to the house, and I grabbed my Winchester and began firing at them from the window, when they broke and ran, but left one man on the ground with a bullet hole through his heart.

I bid my good friends good-bye, got on my sorrel horse, and made my way to Fancy Jim's, where I rested several days.

In company with Charley, the cook, I then went to Gonzales, where I met George Tennille and others, who assured me of their lasting friendship and devotion. I heard from Jim Taylor, who was at Bill Jones' house.

I soon found out that I was not even safe in Gonzales County, and that a mob of seventy-five men under the leadership of Rube Brown and Joe Tomlinson now threatened me. Most of my friends were in Kansas, and with a few exceptions, those that remained were badly scared.

About the 20th of June I received a letter from Capt. Waller, who said he was going to send some prisoners to Gonzales, and if they (the guard) were molested or the prisoners released, that he would kill my father and little brother, and probably my wife and child, whom he now held as hostages. These prisoners were men from my Hamilton herd. Their names were J. B. Brosius, Scrap Taylor, Tuggle, and White. I did not know exactly what to do. Of course, I wanted to attack the guard, who were bringing my hands to DeWitt, but still I knew it meant death to my family. I concluded to keep quiet for a few days. I had about twenty men camped with me at Neal Bowens', my father-in-law, on Elm Creek, in Gonzales County. I finally came to the conclusion that I had better leave the country as soon as I could sell my cattle in Kansas. My money was running low, though I still had the $250 that Mrs. Nix had given me. I employed my father-in-law to go to Kansas, sell my cattle, and return as quickly as possible. When the Rangers got down to Clifton with my hands, they found that there were no charges against them, but learnt that the Tomlinson crowd were eager to kill them. They placed them in jail for that purpose, but nominally to hold them in event of some charges. On the night of the 30th of June these Rangers turned over to the Tomlinson mob Scrap Taylor, Tuggle, and White, who put them all to death by hanging, Dr. J. B. Brosius escaping. On the morning of July 1, 1874, these eighteen Rangers, whose hands were still bloody with the blood of my friends, made a raid on me, but, after a skirmish, they got frightened and left on short order, leaving a dead Ranger behind them. I then went towards Gonzales to see Jim Taylor, but got afraid of Bill Jones' intentions towards me and did not go there.

I went to Tip Davis' near Gonzales and stayed there two days. Then Mac Young and I bid our friends good-bye.

George Tennille went part of the way with us, and when we bid him good-bye it was for the last time.

Mac Young lived at Hempstead, and it was our intention to go there and take the cars for Kansas, shipping our horses also.

One evening about sundown we passed through Bellville, in Austin County, and went out to an old German's about two miles from town, on the Hempstead road. We had just stopped to get supper when a party under Sheriff Langhamer ran on us. It appeared that this old German had suspected us of being horse thieves and had sent to Brenham for officers to arrest us and had held back the serving of the supper until the sheriff and party arrived. They then told us that supper was ready, and as we sat at the table I heard someone open a cap box. I at once pulled one of my pistols out and put it in my lap, winking at Mac. About that time four or five men showed up with double-barreled shotguns, and I covered them with my six-shooter, demanding what they wanted. I told them if they did not at once turn their backs, I would kill the last one of them, and when they turned to go, I went, too, and Mac followed me into the corn patch.

After we had been down there several minutes, I saw

about twelve men coming towards us, about 50 yards off, and one man in front, about ten steps away. I told the man riding in front to halt those men or he was a dead man. He called to them, and they halted. I asked him who he was, and he said his name was Langhamer and that he was sheriff of the county.

By this time Mac and I both had him covered and I had his horse (they having cut us off from ours).

I said, "If you are sheriff, read your warrant for my arrest."

He said, "I have no warrant for you."

"Well," he said, "if you are a law-abiding man, give up, surrender to an officer."

He said, "I arrest you in the name of the State of Texas for unlawfully carrying arms."

I said: "You will play h—— arresting me. I am a law-abiding citizen, and have as much right to carry arms while traveling as you have."

"Well," he said, "if you are a law-abiding man, give up your pistol."

By this time I was a little bit mad and told Mac to pull him off his horse, and if he resisted I would kill him.

Then he begged me not to kill him and said he would give up his horse and pistol. I got on and rode off safely, leaving Mac to the sheriff and posse, who arrested him on charge of carrying a pistol, for which he was fined $100, although he proved himself to be a traveler.

I rode on to my uncle's at Brenham that night, and in a few days Mac came up to see me, with his usual grin.

I abandoned my trip to Kansas as impracticable, and had sent J. D. Hardin of Brenham up there to help sell the herd. He came back in two weeks and brought me $500, saying that Bowen, my father-in-law, was not willing to sell yet. I wrote to Bowen to sell at once and come home, as I had determined to leave the country. Bowen soon did as directed and came home.

I again went to Gonzales County, saw him, and settled all of my cow debts.

I was now about to leave, not because I was an outlaw, but because mob law had become supreme in Texas, as the hanging of my relatives and friends amply proved.

I went to Brenham after my loving wife, who was as true to me as the magnet of steel, met all my friends once more, and settled my business there, preparatory to leaving the country.

Mac Young and I then went to New Orleans by land, and I there rejoined my wife and baby. Harry Swain and wife of Brenham (of which town he was marshal) accompanied them there. Harry had married Jenny Parks, and Hardin, a cousin of mine, Molly Parks; hence the friendship.

After stopping a week or so in New Orleans, my wife, baby, and myself took the steamboat and went to Cedar Keys; then we went to Gainesville, and there I went into the saloon business.

I bought out Sam Burnet's saloon, and the first morning I opened, Bill McCulloch and Frank Harper, stockmen from Texas, walked in. I saw at once that both men recognized me, for I had punched cows with them both. We shook hands and they promised never to say anything about having seen me or knowing my alias. I had adopted the name of Swain, in honor of the marshal of Brenham, who was my friend and always had been.

I stayed in that business until the third day after I had opened, when the marshal of Gainesville, having arrested a Negro, was attacked by a mob on his way to jail.

110

I ran up and asked Wilson if he needed help. He said, "Yes, I summon you, Swain, to assist me in my legal duties."

A big black Negro asked me what I had to do with it, and I knocked him down. I shot another and told the rest to stand back. Just at that time Dr. Cromwell, a Kentuckian, came up with a double-barreled shotgun, and we landed that whole mob in jail, except the one I had knocked down and the one I had shot. This happened about the 1st of May, 1874.

A few days after this, the Negro, Eli, who had caused the above disturbance, attempted to rape a respectable white lady, for which he was arrested and placed in jail. Some of us went to that jail at midnight, set it on fire, and burned Eli with it. The Negroes were very much excited over the burning, but the coroner set everything all right by declaring that Eli had burned himself up in setting the jail on fire. The coroner himself, by the way, was one of our party the night before.

McCulloch and Harper soon came to me and offered to sell them out, as they had not yet done. I did so, and they went back home in January, 1875. I then sold out the most of my saloon and moved to Micanopy, eighteen miles from Gainesville, Fla.

There I set up another bar and traded in horses. I soon sold out, but, in the meantime, had gone to Jacksonville, Fla., and had entered into a contract to furnish 150 beef cattle to Haddock & Co., butchers. It was not long before I had the beef cattle at Jacksonville, but Bill Haddock had just died. The firm refused to take the cattle, so I went into the butcher and liquor business. I sold out my saloon interests in May, 1875, finding that butchering and shipping cattle would consume all my time.

I continued in the cattle business, butchering and shipping, until the middle of April, when two Pinkerton detectives came to Florida and found me out. In the meantime, however, I had gotten well acquainted with the sheriff and marshal and they were my friends and they "put me on" to the Pinkertons.

I at once concluded to leave Jacksonville, and a policeman named Gus Kenedy was to go with me. We went to New Orleans, intending to go to old Mexico, but the Pinkertons followed and came up on us near the line of Florida and Georgia. A fight was the natural result, and two of the Pinkerton gang were killed. I escaped without a scratch.

It had been arranged that my wife and children were to meet me at Eufaula, in Alabama, but on account of the fight with the Pinkertons I was behind time. When I arrived, I found that my beloved wife had fulfilled her part of the engagement, as I saw her name, Mrs. J. H. Swain and children, on the hotel register. On inquiry I found that she had gone to Polland, Alabama, where she had some relatives. We had agreed on this plan in case I could not meet her. I took the night train for Polland, and there met my beloved wife and two children, Molly and John W. Hardin.

After stopping there about a week we concluded to go to Tuxpan, and we started for that place about the 20th of August, 1876. When we arrived at East Poseugoula, we found that we would be quarantined as being from New Orleans, where yellow fever had broken out. So I stopped at Poseugoula to await the raising of the quarantine.

Then Gus and I went back to Mobile to play poker and cards, and we were so successful as to win about $3,500. We would go back and forward between Poseugoula and Mobile.

The presidential election was on while we were in Mobile, and on that day all the gambling fraternity there got on a high lonesome and took in the town. One of our party got into a row, and of course I took a hand. The row started in a house where I had ordered some wine, but instead they brought beer. I was mad at this and kicked the table over, and the waiter yelled loud enough to awake the echoes. A row followed with Cliff Lewis, which soon became general. I did all in my power to stop it but failed. Our party got out in the streets, and the party in the house (composed mostly of city police) began firing on us and advancing. We now answered their fire, and after killing two and wounding another, we drove them back into the house. No one saw me shoot except Gus, and no one saw Gus shoot except me. We then ran down a street and I threw my .45 Colt's over into a yard and told Gus to do likewise, as we expected to give up if we were arrested. We went to a coffee house and ordered coffee. While drinking it, four or five policemen came in and arrested Gus and myself. They took us to the lock-up and told us we were arrested for murder. We, of course, denied being present at all while the shooting was going on. Finally, after spending three or four days in jail and spending $2,500, we got a hearing and were discharged. The proprietors of the house testified that I had done everything possible to keep down the row and that Gus and I had left before the shooting took place. Gus had been arrested, to my surprise, for having a pistol (which I had told him to throw away), three barrels of which had been discharged. Money, however, made this very easily explained in court.

I then went to Poseugoula, got my wife and children, and went back to Polland, Alabama. We went out into the country south of Polland and stayed there with an uncle of my wife's.

Soon afterwards I concluded to go into the logging business and formed a partnership with a man named Shep Hardie, who was an experienced logger. We went west about sixty miles to the Stick River and began, doing well.

In the meantime, Brown Bowen, a brother of my wife's, under several indictments for murder, came to Polland. He wrote a letter home to my father-in-law, Neal Bowen, in Gonzales County on Elm Creek, and said that my wife (his sister) joined him in sending love. At the time Neal Bowen received the letter, Lieutenant Armstrong of the Rangers was situated at Cuero to see if he could detect my whereabouts. He had sent Jack Duncan, a special Ranger, to my father-in-law's house. Jack pretended to be in some trouble and decided to buy a small grocery store from Neal Bowen, and went so far as to take stock.

One day Jack and Neal had gone to Rancho and Jack noticed that Neal got a letter which he put in his trunk when he got home. When Neal left the house, Jack opened the trunk and got the letter that gave him the information he wanted, although he (my wife's brother) only stated that he had joined his sister in love to their father.

Neal answered the letter at once and in it mentioned some litigation which he was involved in over my property. He addressed the letter to me, J. H. Swain, Polland, Alabama, in care of Neal McMellon, sheriff of Escambia County.

Now Neal McMellon was a kinsman of my wife's and the letter Bowen wrote, which Jack got out of the trunk, mentioned this fact. When Neal had written the letter, he asked the pretended storekeeper for an envelope, which he gave him, but secretly marked the envelope. Neal and Jack went to Rancho to get some supplies and mail the letter. Neal went to the post office with Jack and mailed the letter.

Neal stepped out to buy supplies, when Jack told the postmaster he would like to get a letter back out of the office which he had just mailed and described it. He said he wished to make some alterations in it, and the unsuspecting postmaster gave it to him. Jack opened the letter, stepped aside, and read it. He saw at once that he had the information he wanted. He wrote to Armstrong to "come and get his horse." Armstrong came up to Coon Hollow, arrested the pretended storekeeper, placed him in irons, and brought him to Cuero in a wagon.

When they got to Cuero, they took the first train to Austin and consulted Dick Hubbard, the governor of Texas, as to extraditing me. After this they struck out for Polland, Alabama.

Jack came ahead and stopped at Pensacola Junction, eight miles from Polland, about the 18th of July, 1877. I was at this time over on the Stock River, about sixty miles away, but Brown Bowen was in the vicinity of the junction and came there every day.

On or about the 19th of July, Bowen got on a spree and got into a row with Mr. Shipley, the general manager of the railroad. He got the worst of the row and the next day came back to the junction, vowing vengeance. He said that when I came back, I would wake things up; that I was not the peaceable John Swain everybody thought I was, but that I was the notorious John Wesley Hardin. Of course, such talk as this inflamed the minds of Shipley and his friends.

About this time my partner and myself concluded to go to Pensacola to buy our supplies, and, of course, to play some cards. Now Shep was in the habit of going to Pensacola and blowing in his earnings. He was thus well acquainted and introduced me as his friend. We all soon got into a poker game, Shipley and I having a system understood between us which proved a winner. It was all I could do to keep Shipley from getting too drunk for us to win the money. About the 22nd of July I shipped some groceries to the Junction for home consumption from Pensacola. Thus Shipley was able to tell Jack Duncan where I was, and furnished him an extra train to go there at once. When he came, he soon located me in the poker room, but was afraid to tackle me there. So, after spending the night watching me without daring to make a break, he went to the sheriff and told him that I would take the train that evening, the 23rd of July, 1877, and if he would arrest me alive, he would give him $500. The sheriff consented to this, and in due time I went to the train with my friends, Shep Hardie and Neal Campbell, Jim Man, and two or three others. At that time I was in the habit of smoking a pipe, and we all took the smoking car, not knowing that I was soon to be attacked. The car was standing close to the hotel, the gallery or portico of which ran parallel with the car. Duncan and the sheriff had placed twenty men in the rooms opening on this veranda to be ready for action in a moment's notice. Jack Duncan commanded these, and they were stationed immediately above the car and within 25 feet of me, who, with my companions, was all unconscious of the impending danger. Armstrong was to work in the car below, and took his stand in the express or baggage car next to the smoker. Finally I saw the high sheriff and deputies come through the car and pass out. Then another deputy came in whom I had played cards with and from whom I had won $150 or $200. He said, "Swain, can't you stop over. I have got a roll here and if you can beat me, you can have it."

I said, "Business before pleasure; I can't stop over."

"Well," said he, "we fellows played you for a sucker and got left. You seem a gentleman; come down again and we'll give you a nice game and won't play you for a green-horn any more."

I told him I was very fond of the game and had been very lucky, and hoped at some future time to meet him and his friends over the green cloth. I told him it was a case of business before pleasure with me now and remarked that when I held a good hand, I couldnt lay them down.

"Yes," said he, "and you seem to hold them oftener than any one else I ever played with."

We said good-bye and shook hands and I kept smoking my meerschaum pipe. In a minute the sheriff and a deputy (either of whom would weigh 170 or 180 pounds) came in at the door behind me and grabbed me, saying, "Surrender! Hold up your hands."

I asked them what it all meant and appeared amazed. I hollered, "Robbers! Protect me."

I wanted to throw them off their guard or a diversion for a second or two.

Had they done so, I would have gotten my pistol. At this moment the deputy who had just bidden me good-bye came in and asked what was the matter. I said, "You know I have done nothing; protect me."

He pretended to do so, but instead caught hold of my legs and threw me down in the aisle. A terrible struggle was now going on, and the party from the gallery fired a volley into the car. Jim Man, a young man 19 years old, jumped up and passed over me, struggling in the aisle, and rushed to the north end of the smoker, where he was met by Armstrong and others, who shot him dead. He jumped out of a window and fell dead, pierced by several fatal balls. In the meantime I was fighting for liberty in the aisle with my three antagonists, who had been reinforced. They had me on my back, two or three men clinging to each arm, some on my breast, and others trying to catch my legs, which I was using with a vim. Once in a while they would hit me over the head with a six-shooter as the unequal fight went on. I would not surrender, or keep still. I swore I would never surrender at the point of a pistol, and I was not going to do it now. At this time Armstrong rushed into the smoker with a drawn revolver and put it to my head and told me if I did not surrender he would blow my brains out. I said, "Blow away. You will never blow a more innocent man's out, or one that will care less."

Someone else was trying to strike me over the head with a revolver when Armstrong called out, "Men, we have him now; don't hurt him; he is too brave to kill, and the first man that shoots him I'll kill him."

They finally bound me with my hands behind my back with a big cable, and then tied me to the seat of the car. I still had the stem of my pipe in my mouth and someone picked up the bowl, filled it, lit it, and gave it to me to smoke.

When Jack saw I was fast, he came down from his perch and slapped me on the back, saying, "John, take a cigar. Oh yes," he said, "John Wesley Hardin, you are the worst man in the country, but we have got you at last."

I said, "Stranger, what asylum are you from?"

He said he was from Texas and was only feeling good over the capture of the notorious John Wesley Hardin. He said to Armstrong and others standing by, "Have you taken his pistol?"

They replied no, that I had no gun. Jack Duncan said, "That's too thin," and ran his hand between my over and

THE ARREST AT PENSACOLA

undershirt, pulling out a .44 Colt's cap-and-ball six-shooter, remarking to the others, "What did I tell you?"

The train pulled out for the Junction, and I kept demanding to see the warrant for my arrest and by what legal right they had killed Jim Man and captured me. I told the sheriff that I wanted protection from these Texas kidnappers, but to all this they made no reply.

Oh, that was one time I wanted to die but could not. I remembered how my own brother and relatives had been led out of the courthouse at Comanche, bareheaded and barefooted, and hung by a mob. I felt as if a similar death awaited me, so I wanted to die now, but could not. I had the glad consciousness, however, of knowing that I had done all that courage and strength could do and that I had kept my oath never to surrender at the point of a pistol. Thus was my arrest accomplished on the 23rd of July, 1877.

We soon arrived at the Junction, and there I sent my loving wife some money. In the meantime my friends at Polland, eight miles away, had formed a rescuing party with the sheriff at their head and expected to legally release me when the train came through Polland, as it generally stopped there several minutes. But unfortunately the train passed through without stopping, and they went on to Mobile, where they placed me in jail and went off to sleep.

This was now the 24th day of July, and I sent for an attorney. Young Watts came, and after I had told him my case, he took it. He guaranteed to release me for $500. He got out a writ of habeas corpus, and they were in the act of turning me loose when Jack Duncan and Armstrong came up and changed the whole business by securing a continuance.

In the meantime Dick Hubbard of Texas had telegraphed

to the governor of Alabama to hold me, as requisition papers were on the way.

On the night of the 24th these papers came, and on the morning of the 25th we started for Texas. My wife and friends were still on the alert and a party of nine men were ready there at the depot to rescue me. But the wily Jack Duncan took a hack and carried me to a station several miles from Montgomery, and we again took the train for Texas. He thus avoided a collision with my friends.

I knew my only hope now was to escape. My guards were kind to me, but they were most vigilant. By promising to be quiet I had caused them to relax somewhat, and they appeared anxious to treat me kindly, but they knew their life depended on how they used me. When we got to a little town, I think it was Decatur, we had to stop and change cars for Memphis. They took me to an hotel, got a room, and sent for our meals. Jack and Armstrong were now getting intimate with me, and when dinner came I suggested the necessity of removing my cuffs and they agreed to do so. Armstrong unlocked the jewelry and started to turn around, exposing his six-shooter to me, when Jack jerked him around and pulled his pistol at the same time. "Look out," he said, "John will kill us and escape." Of course, I laughed at him and ridiculed the idea. It was really the very chance I was looking for, but Jack had taken the play away just before it got ripe. I intended to jerk Armstrong's pistol, kill Jack Duncan or make him throw up his hands. I could have made him unlock my shackles, or get the key from his dead body and do it myself. I could then have easily made my escape. That time never came again.

We again struck out for Texas and stopped at Memphis, where they put me in jail. We took the train again for

Texas by way of Little Rock, and by this time our car was beseiged by people who had read the account of my capture. It had been the same way at Memphis, where people flocked to the jail to see me in such numbers that it took a squad of policemen to keep them back. One man named Roe actually rode from Memphis to Texarkana to see me, and his wish was gratified by these gallant officers, who brought him into the sleeper where I was trying to rest.

"Why," he said, "there is nothing bad in your face. Your life has been misrepresented to me. Here is $50. Take it from a sympathizer."

I thanked him and he bid me good-bye.

At every station on to Austin a crowd of curious people were at the depot to see me, but I was so well guarded that few succeeded.

When we got to Austin, my guards learned that there was a tremendous crowd at the depot, and so they stopped the train and took a hack for the jail. The crowd at the depot learned of the move and broke for the jail. The hack just did manage to get there first, and they carried me bodily into the jail; so when the crowd arrived, they failed to see the great curiosity.

I wrote to some of my relatives at once and to my friends, many of whom I had not seen for four years. Most of them responded and generously came to my assistance with influence and means.

I stayed in Austin jail until the latter part of September, and then a company of Rangers (No. 35) commanded by N. O. Reynolds and accompanied by Sheriff Wilson and his deputies escorted me to Comanche.

The reason I was guarded by such a strong escort was because they were afraid that the brutal mob who had hung my relatives would hang me.

122

After traveling several days we reached Comanche, about 160 miles from Austin. Of course, our military appearance created interest in every town through which we passed. I rode in a buggy with Sheriff Wilson, the most of the company in front and the lesser part bringing up the rear. We camped out every night and my escort did everything in their power to make me comfortable, except that they kept me securely shackled and cuffed. On arriving at Comanche, my escort marched up, waited for me to be carried into the jail, as I was too heavily shackled to walk. Reynolds placed a guard around the jail and went out to see what the situation was. He soon found that feeling was very violent against me and that there were 200 men camped two miles from town for the purpose of hanging me.

The sheriff had summoned thirty-five citizens to guard me in the jail. Knowing the situation, and feeling somewhat interested, I told Lieutenant Reynolds to put the citizens outside the jail yard to guard me and his men inside if he wished to save me. He wisely did this. My idea was that if the mob made an attack on the jail the citizen guard would assist them and if they were inside they would overpower the Rangers, which they could not do if they were separated.

The brave Reynolds told me that if the mob attacked me or the jail, he would arm me and let me out to rough it with him and his men. He would also arm the men in jail, of whom there were ten or twelve. He gave this out publicly, and the move never came, but I received anonymous letters saying that if I put off my trial or got a change of venue, they would make a demand for me.

As I did not have the confidence in the Rangers I should have had, I announced ready for trial. I considered a "demand" equal to a delivery to the mob, for I had wrongly no confidence in the Rangers. I remembered how my own brother and relatives had been hung by a mob and when there was a company of Rangers in the town at the time and ten of them actually on duty.

I employed to defend me S. H. Renick of Waco, T. L. Nugent of Stephenville, and Adams of Comanche. Either from fear of the mob or some other unknown cause my counsel allowed the State to put in evidence my character to influence the jury without raising any objection. The very judge himself was disqualified and biased. He had actually given counsel to Frank Wilson about my arrest just before the killing of Webb. He was plainly disqualified. They never allowed any evidence of my escape to be brought up, although I could easily have shown that I gave up to the sheriff in good faith and only escaped when the mob disarmed the sheriff, fired on me, and finally hung my brother and cousins.

The State tried to prove a conspiracy, but utterly failed in this, hence the prosecution ought to have fallen through. The State proved themselves that Charley Webb had fired at me twice before I drew my pistol, or that I drew and fired as he was shooting his second shot.

The simple fact is that Charles Webb had really come over from his own county that day to kill me, thinking I was drinking and at a disadvantage. He wanted to kill me to keep his name, and he made his break on me like an assassin would. He fired his first shot at my vitals when I was unprepared, and who blames a man for shooting under such conditions? I was at a terrible disadvantage in my trial. I went before the court on a charge of murder without a witness. The cowardly mob had either killed them or run them out of the county. I went to trial in a town in which three years before my own brother and cousins

124

had met an awful death at the hands of a mob. Who of my readers would like to be tried under these circumstances? On that jury that tried me sat six men whom I knew to be directly implicated in my brother's death. No, my readers, I have served twenty-five years for the killing of Webb, but know ye that there is a God in high heaven who knows that I did not shoot Charles Webb through malice, nor through anger, nor for money, but to save my own life.

True, it is almost as bad to kill as to be killed. It drove my father to an early grave; it almost distracted my mother; it killed my brother Joe and my cousins Tom and William; it left my brother's widow with two helpless babes; Mrs. Anderson lost her son Ham, and Mrs. Susan Barrickman lost her husband, to say nothing of the grief of countless others. I do say, however, that the man who does not exercise the first law of nature—that of self preservation—is not worthy of living and breathing the breath of life.

The jury gave me twenty-five years in the penitentiary and found me guilty of murder in the second degree. I appealed the case. The Rangers took me back to Austin to await the result of my appeal. Judge White affirmed the decision of the lower court, and they took me back to Comanche in the latter part of September, 1878, where I received my sentence of twenty-five years with hard labor.

While I was in that Austin jail, I had done everything in my power to escape. The cells were made of good material and in fact the jail was a good one, with one set of cages on top of the others, separated by sheet iron. I soon got so I could make a key that would unlock my cell door and put me in the run-around. I made a key to unlock that, and now all I had to do was climb to the window and saw one of the bars. I could then easily escape. But some "trusties" found out the scheme and gave it away to the jailer, who placed a guard inside the jail day and night. Thus it became impossible for me to do the work in the window, though I had the key to the cell and the run-around.

There were from sixty to ninety prisoners in that jail all the time, and at least fifty of these stood ready to inform on me any time. There was the trouble about getting out.

In that jail I met some noted men. Bill Taylor, George Gladden, John Ringo, Manning Clements, Pipes and Herndon of the Bass gang, John Collins, Jeff Ake, and Brown Bowen.

After receiving my sentence at Comanche, they started with me to Huntsville, shackled to John Maston, a blacksmith of Comanche convicted of attempting to murder and under two years' sentence. This man afterwards committed suicide by jumping from the upper story in the building to a Rock floor, where he was dashed to pieces. Nat Mackey, who was sentenced for seventeen years for killing a man with a rock, was chained to Davenport, who had a sentence of five years for horse stealing. Thus there were four prisoners chained by two's in a wagon and guarded by a sheriff and company of Rangers. Of course, great crowds would flock from everywhere to see the notorious John Wesley Hardin, from the hoary-headed farmer to the little maid hardly in her teens.

On one occasion a young lady told me she had come over to where we were passing the day before and would not have missed seeing me for $100. I asked her if she was satisfied now. She said, "Oh, yes; I can tell everybody I have seen the notorious John Wesley Hardin, and he is so handsome!"

126

I said, "Yes, my wife thinks so."

When we got to Fort Worth, the people turned out like a Fourth of July picnic, and I had to get out of the wagon and shake hands for an hour before my guard could get me through the crowd.

We stopped at Fort Worth all day and all night and then took the train for Huntsville. We arrived there on the 5th of October, 1878, and crowds would come all along the route to see us, especially at Palestine. I was astonished to see even the convicts in stripes gazing at me when we got inside the walls of the penitentiary.

Then they gave me a breakfast of coffee, bacon, bread, and molasses, shaved me smooth, cut my hair, and weighed me. I tipped the scale at 165 pounds. Then they gave me a bath and took down all the scars and marks on my body. They asked me what my occupation was and assigned me to the wheelwright's shop.

I knew there were a heap of Judases and Benedict Arnolds in the world and had had a lifelong experience with the meaning of the word treachery. I believed, however, that in jail even a coward was a brave man, so I went to work to plan my escape.

I found out where the armory was, about 75 yards off from the wheelwright's shop, and concluded to undermine towards it. A carpenter's shop, the superintendent's and director's office had to be undermined before we got there. I took into the conspiracy about seventy-five of the best men, mostly life and long-term men. Only those who were to do the actual work were let into the plan, the rest were to blindly trust me to say the word and then follow me. The plan was to reach the armory by the underground passage and there wait until the guards came in to put up their guns and went to eat their supper. We would then seize the guns, demand a surrender, take the prison, and liberate all who wished to go except the rape fiends. I perfected my plans about the 1st of November and we began to tunnel towards the armory. We had to tunnel through five brick walls twenty-four inches thick. This we easily did for we had saw bits, chisels, and almost every tool adapted to such work. We were working from the wheelwright's shop, and while one would work, the others would watch. We used a small rope or cord as a signal. If the man working wanted any tools, he would give a signal. By pulling the rope, we would find a note on the end of it telling anything he wished to say.

So we finished our work quickly, and about the 20th of November we were waiting for the guards to put up their guns before cutting through the pine floor. These guards were in the habit of taking outside the walls from 100 to 150 to work on the outside, and it was when these guards came in to their supper that we intended to make our break. Meanwhile, several life convicts rushed to the superintendent's office, told him of the conspiracy and how near it was being executed. The superintendent arrested me and nine others, putting us in irons. When I denied all knowledge of the armory conspiracy, they put me in a dark cell on bread and water for fifteen days, with a ball and chain attachment.

There were twelve of us doing the tunneling. Two told it to the authorities and "on pressure" nine others owned up. I am certain two long-time men were pardoned, Bill Owens and Bill Terril from Waco, the latter having a twenty-five-year sentence. I believe that three others got their time cut for the same reason—betraying the plot.

When they took me out of the dark cell, they put me to work in the factory. I was now "celling" with a lifetime man named John Williams and he was the turnkey on our row. He was in with me on the tunneling scheme and had played traitor, although I was not aware of it.

I now conceived the plan of making keys to all the cells on our row, in which there were some eighteen or twenty cells all locked with padlocks. I soon had the keys ready and also had impressions of the keys to the outer gates of the prison and had made keys to them which worked well.

For some time I had been able to dispense with my ball and chain. I had cut the brads off that held the shackles together and had put on instead a bolt with a tap on it, which I could unscrew at will.

On the 26th of December I gave John Williams the keys to see if they would work and he said they worked like a charm. I intended on the night of the 26th to unlock my door and then all the other cells, muzzle the guard, unlock the main prison door and then gate after gate to freedom. I determined to resist all opposition and had two good six-shooters that a trusty had brought in to me for that purpose. That evening I was suddenly arrested and locked up. They searched me, found my keys and also the bolt in my shackles; in short, my cell mate had betrayed me and the game was up.

That night about twenty officers came in and tied my hands and feet. They jerked me down upon a concrete floor and stretched me out upon my face. Two men got hold of the ropes that held my hands and two more of the ropes that held my feet. Then the underkeeper, West, took a strap about 20 inches long and 2 1-4 inches thick. It was attached to a handle about 12 inches long. He began to whip my naked body with this instrument. They were now flogging me and every lick left the imprint of every lash, of which there were four in this whip, consisting of thick pieces of thick harness leather. I heard some one say, "Don't hit him in the same place so often."

At last the superintendent said, "That will do," after they had hit me thirty-nine lashes, the limit.

My sides and back were beaten into a jelly, and, still quivering and bleeding, they made me walk in the snow across to another building, where they placed me in a dark cell and threatened to starve me to death if I did not reveal the plot. I told them I would tell them nothing; that I meant to escape and would kill them in a minute if they stood in my way. They left me there for three days without anything to eat or drink, and on the fourth day I was carried to another cell in a high fever and unable to walk. I stayed there for thirty days.

About the 1st of February, 1879, they took me out and put me to work in the wood shop. All this time I was plotting and scheming to get away, but my fellow convicts always gave me away and generally got some privilege for doing so. I was not able to do the work in the wood shop and was in a row all the time with the guard, who had orders to watch and work me. He did not work me much, for when he told me to take hold of a plank, I told him I couldn't without hurting myself and would refer him to the doctor. He would sometimes report me, but that did no good as I would sooner have taken the punishment than worked there.

In June, 1879, I was put to work in the boot and shoe shop at my own solicitation and soon became one of the best fitters and cutters they ever had.

By this time I began to realize how much of a traitor the average convict was to his fellow. I concluded to try bribing a guard, which I succeeded in doing. Jim Hall, the man who killed Marshal Gosling, was in this plot. Well, to cut a long story short, we got out into the prison yard, when thirty armed men arrested us and took us to the dark cells. This plot was also given away by a convict.

They flogged me again, but not so cruelly as before. I concluded I could make no play that the officers would not get on to and was more cautious from that on. My desire to escape was as strong as ever.

I was getting along tolerably well for a man in prison and began reading a good deal. I managed my work so as to make it very light, and took up arithmetic and mathematics as a study. I went through Stoddard's arithmetic and Davies' algebra and geometry; the balance of my time I devoted to history.

One night the officers came to my cell and told me to come out. They tied me and flogged me again for some imaginary crime and flogged about thirty others for nothing. They may have done this to scare me.

Now I wanted to get away worse than ever before. I became more and more prudent in my actions and conversations and began getting along all right once more.

I had now been working in the shop since July, 1879, and this was 1883.

Then three other convicts and I conceived the idea of attacking the southwest picket with pistols and trying to climb the walls, but we had finally to give this up because we could not get the firearms. Still & Co. were running a saddle shop in the walls, and this shop ran close to the picket spoken of. Eugene Hall was working in this shop, and Still & Co. were constantly receiving boxes of material by express. Eugene Hall and I were friends, and he was as anxious to escape as I was. Every Sunday we would compare notes. I asked him one Sunday if he had a friend outside who could be induced to box up some arms and

131

send them to us. He said he thought he had. I told him to tell his friend to box them up in a black box and send them by express to Still & Co. We knew we could see if the black box came when the whistle blew and we all went out to dinner. We intended to get the guns and fight our way out. Hall's friend weakened, however, and that game was up for the present.

In the meantime Bud Bohannon had been assigned to Still & Co., and not trusting the man very much, but knowing he wanted to escape, I told Hall to approach him and see if he favored my plan, but telling Hall not to mention my name. Bohannon liked my plan and at once began to execute it. Of course I was in the play, but talked to no one but Hall on the subject. On the Sunday before it was all to come off, I saw Hall and told him that I would take one six-shooter and throw down on the guard from the southwest window of the shop and tell him that his life depended on his actions. If he did not obey, I would kill him, the distance being only about ten yards. I then wanted him and his pals to go up a ladder, take him and his arms away and await me at the picket. Then we were to go to the State stable, get horses, and leave. Of course, I said, we may have the guard to kill and we are very apt to have some fighting to do, but we can do it so quickly that not even the prisoners need know it, much less the town. That was my plan.

Bohannon wanted to attack the gate keeper and make him open the gate. This was not feasible. Then he wanted to climb the walls with ladders at a place not practicable. Besides all this, he wanted to go and hunt up other men to make the play after he and Hall got the guns.

I told Eugene Hall I would have no more to do with it unless the men who were in the play would watch the ex-

132

press wagon and go at once to Still & Co.'s to get the pistols. They must then attack the southwest picket. Hall told me that Bohannon would not do that, so I drew out of it.

Sure enough, when the time came, I saw the black box come in, and in a few moments Bohannon came by me and offered me a pistol. I declined it. I saw three or four convicts out in the yard rushing here and there aimlessly. They went to the gate, but the gate keeper, being on the outside, got out of their way. They had no certain plan of action and fired several shots either in the air or at the pickets. They finally surrendered before reaching the walls. Of course, they whipped them.

I kept on working in the shoe shop until the fall of 1883, when I was taken sick with an abcess in my side and had to give up work. I had been shot in 1872 in my side and this was the wound that became affected.

The officials made fun of me and treated me cruelly. I was denied a place in the hospital, but had a nurse and was permitted to stay in my cell. For eight months it looked as if I never would get well, but finally I began to slowly improve, and when I was able to walk, Assistant Superintendent Ben McCulloch wanted me to go to work again, but I refused because I was not able to do so.

After a few days he locked me up on bread and water. When he finally turned me out, I went to work in the tailor shop. They put me to work making quilts. I got the guard and foreman to give me a certain task and got permission to read when I had finished it.

I was now a constant reader. In the years 1880, 1881, 1882, I had studied theology and had been superintendent of our Sunday School. We had a debating society there, of which I was a member and had been president.

In 1885 I conceived the idea of studying law and wrote

to the superintendent asking for his advice about what to read in order to have a practical knowledge of both civil and criminal law. He referred this letter to Col. A. T. Mc-Kinney of the Huntsville bar. In a few days I received the following letter:

Huntsville, 6th May, 1889.

Hon. Thos. J. Goree:

Dear Sir—Replying to your favor covering note of Mr. John Wesley Hardin, I beg to state that applicants for license under the rules of the Supreme Court are usually examined on the following books:

Blackstone's Commentaries, 4 vols.
Kent's, 4 vols.
Stephens on Pleading, 1 vol.
Storey's Equity, 2 vols.
Greenleaf on Evidence, 1 vol.
Parsons on Contracts, 3 vols.
Daniels on Negotiable Instruments, 2 vols.
Storey on Partnership, 1 vol.
Storey's Equity Jurisprudence, 2 vols.
Revised Statutes of Texas, 1 vol.

For a person who desires to pay special attention to criminal jurisprudence, I would advise him to read Walker's Introduction to American Law, 1 vol., and Bishop's Criminal Law, 2 vols., before reading the course recommended by our Supreme Court.

These books (except the Revised Statutes) can be obtained at about $6 per volume from T. H. Thomas & Co., of St. Louis. The Revised Statutes can be obtained from the secretary of State, Hon. J. M. Moore, Austin, Texas, for $2.50. Yours truly,

A. T. M'KINNEY.

[*Here abruptly ends the Hardin manuscript—Publishers.*]

APPENDIX

———

Some idea of the Hardin of 1881 in the state prison at Huntsville may be gleaned from letters written to his wife. In one of them he says, (July, 1881). "It is now about 8 o'clock P.M. and I am locked into my cell for the night. By special permission from my keeper I now write you. I can tell you that I spent this day in almost perfect happiness, as I generally spend the Sabbaths here, something that I once could not enjoy because I did not know the causes or results of that day. I had no idea before how it benefits a man in my condition. Although we are all prisoners here we are on the road to progress. "J. S." and I are both members of our societies and we are looked upon as the leaders by our associates, of which we have a goodly number. John is president of the Moral and Christian Society and I am secretary of our Debating Club. I spoke in our debating club this evening on the subject of Woman's Rights. John held that women should have equal rights with men and I held they shouldn't. We had a lively time. I followed him, winding up the debate for the day. John is the champion of woman's rights, but he failed to convince the judges, who after they had listened to my argument, decided in my favor," etc.

The following is a copy of the pardon and restoration to citizenship granted to Hardin by Governor Hogg:

By the Governor of the State of Texas

To All to Whom These Presents Shall Come:

Whereas, at the spring term, A.D. 1878 in the district court of Comanche County, State of Texas, John Wesley Hardin was convicted of murder in the second degree and sentenced to the Penitentiary for twenty-five years; concurrent with which sentence is a sentence for two years in the district court of DeWitt county, Texas, January 1st, 1892, for manslaughter, and

Whereas, For the reason that he has served out his term of sentence and was discharged from the penitentiary on the 17th day of February, 1894, that good citizens ask it;

Now, therefore, I, J. S. Hogg, Governor of Texas, do by virtue of the authority vested in me by the constitution and laws of this State, hereby, for the reasons specified, now on file in the office of the Secretary of State, do grant to said convict, John Wesley Hardin, full pardon in both cases and restore him to full citizenship and the right of suffrage.

In testimony whereof I have hereto signed my name and caused the seal of the State to be affixed at the city of Austin, this 16th day of March, A.D. 1894.

J. S. HOGG, *Governor.*

GEO. W. SMITH, *Secretary of State.*

Hardin, after being released from the penitentiary, joined his children in Gonzales County and finally located in the town of Gonzales, where he entered into the practice of law.

During the exciting political campaign of 1894 he took an active interest in local politics, supporting Coleman against W. E. Jones for sheriff of Gonzales County. A bitter controversy grew out of this between Jones and Hardin, and friends of both parties at one time feared serious trouble between the two men. After the election of Jones, Hardin moved to Karnes County.

Early in 1895 he married Miss Callie Lewis of London, Tex., his first wife having died shortly before his release from prison. Soon after this he moved to El Paso, where he lived until his death.

We publish the following letters from prominent men written to Hardin on his release:

Hon. Barnett Gibbs writes him from Dallas, under date February 18th, 1894:

Dear Sir—I see from the News that you have been pardoned and am glad of it, for, however great your offense, I feel sure that you have in you the making of a useful man. I hope you will adhere to your good resolutions. Many a man has started in life and in law at your present age and made a success. You have my best wishes in your new life and I will at any time be glad to serve you. Lawyers, as a rule, are generous and liberal in their views and I don't think any of them will fail to appreciate your desire to make up the time you have lost in atoning for your offenses against society. If you should come to Dallas, call upon me. Yours respectfully,

BARNETT GIBBS

Judge W. S. Fly, associate justice of the Court of Appeals, in sending him a full pardon from Governor Hogg, writes:

Dear Sir—Enclosed I send you a full pardon from the Governor of Texas. I congratulate you on its reception and trust that it is the day dawn of a bright and peaceful future. There is time to retrieve a lost past. Turn your back upon it with all its suffering and sorrow and fix your eyes upon the future with the determination to make yourself an honorable and useful member of society. The hand of every

137

true man will be extended to assist you in your upward course and I trust that the name of Hardin will in the future be associated with the performance of deeds that will ennoble his family and be a blessing to humanity. Did you ever read Victor Hugo's masterpiece, "Les Miserables"? If not, you ought to read it. It paints in graphic words the life of one who had tasted the bitterest dregs of life's cup, but in his Christian manhood rose above it almost like a god and left behind him a path luminous with good deeds. With the best wishes for your welfare and happiness, I am, yours very truly,

W. S. FLY

Hardin has often been accused of being the real murderer of Thomas Halderman, although Brown Bowen was hung for the crime at Gonzales in 1878. On the scaffold Bowen reiterated his statement that Hardin and not he was the murderer. In a letter written from the Austin jail, May 18, 1878, Hardin writes his wife:

Your pa and Matt came to see me on the 15th. Matt was the same as ever and your pa too. Of course it is reasonable to suppose your pa has done everything he could to save poor Brown, but to no advantage. He is troubled almost to death. He could do nothing. Jane, dearest, I think as much of your pa and family as ever and blame him for nothing, although I have been badly treated. Dear one, on your account and sister Matt's I forgive your pa. He and Matt send their love to you and family. Dear one, your pa wanted to know if there was a statement I could make that would save Brown. I told him no, not an honorable, truthful one, and I told him I hoped he did not want me to make a false one. I told him a true statement would do him no good and a false one I would not make. I told him I would do the best I could, as he insisted that the governor would not allow him even thirty days. So I retired to my cell. They came back the next morning and asked the jailor for the statement. The jailor told me they were there, but I made no reply. In about ten minutes I received the following note:

"Brother John—You told me you would make a true statement about my brother. O, God! why didn't you? O, my God! my poor brother has to be hung. O, my God! do something for him on my account.

MATT E. BOWEN"

I answered her note:

"Dear Sister—My will is good will, but let every tub stand on its own bottom. You ask me to do this for your sake. For your sake I would do anything honorable, but I can not be made a scapegoat of, and a true statement will do your brother no good, and a false one I will not make. Sister, I have a statement already, a true one, and will give it to you or your pa and you can do as you please with it. I am, your sympathizing brother,

JOHN W. HARDIN"

In a letter to his wife just after the hanging of Bowen he said: "Matt nor your father ever called for the paper. Dear, I forgive poor Brown for his false statements, and may God forgive him. Even after the cap was taken off him he said he was innocent but that John Wesley Hardin did it. He then fell seven feet and lived seven seconds. The whole thing was witnessed by 4,500 people. May his poor soul rest in peace and may God forgive his sins."

On June 22nd, 1879, he writes to Manning Clements from Huntsville on the same subject: "As to the report in the Galveston News that I am the murderer of Tom Halderman, I do not consider it worthy of a denial, for I have never had courage to take a man's life as Halderman's was taken. Any one who ever says that I ever said I killed him is a liar and a mischief making scoundrel, and would steal half dollars from his dead mother's eyes for gain. It looks as if some one wants to make a scapegoat of me, but that game won't work."

We publish the following from the El Paso Times of date of April 23rd, 1895. Hardin evidently had a difficult case in the criminal dockets of the El Paso courts. Juárez is the Mexican town just across the Río Grande from El Paso. The Times says: "The toughs who rallied around the imprisoned McRose and Queen in Juárez gave it out that they would bulldoze Attorney John Wesley Hardin if he tried professionally to defeat their schemes to defeat extradition. Last night Mr. Hardin met the gang in Juárez and slapped their faces one after another."

THE DEATH OF HARDIN

THE EL PASO DAILY HERALD of August 20th, 1895, gives the following account of the killing of Hardin:

Last night between 11 and 12 o'clock San Antonio street was thrown into an intense state of excitement by the sound of four pistol shots that occurred at the Acme saloon. Soon the crowd surged against the door, and there, right inside, lay the body of John Wesley Hardin, his blood flowing over the floor and his brains oozing out of a pistol shot wound that had passed through his head. Soon the fact became known that John Selman, constable of Precinct No. 1, had fired the fatal shots that had ended the career of so noted a character as Wes Hardin, by which name he is better known to all old Texans. For several weeks past trouble has been brewing and it has been often heard on the streets that John Wesley Hardin would be the cause of some killing before he left the town.

Only a short time ago Policeman Selman arrested Mrs. McRose, the mistress of Hardin, and she was tried and convicted of carrying a pistol. This angered Hardin and when he was drinking he often made remarks that showed he was bitter in his feelings towards John Selman. Selman paid no attention to these remarks, but attended to his duties and said nothing. Lately Hardin had become louder in his abuse and had continually been under the influence of liquor and at such times he was very quarrelsome, even getting along badly with some of his friends. This quarrelsome disposition on his part resulted in his death last night and it is a sad warning to all such parties that the rights of others must be respected and that the day is past when a person having the name of being a bad man can run rough shod over the law and rights of other citizens. This morning early a Herald reporter started after the facts and found John Selman, the man who fired the fatal shots, and his statement was as follows:

" 'I met Wes Hardin about 7 o'clock last evening close to the Acme saloon. When we met, Hardin said, 'You've got a son that is a bastardly, cowardly s—— of a b——.'

"I said: 'Which one?'

"Hardin said:: 'John, the one that is on the police force. He pulled my woman when I was absent and robbed her of $50, which they would not have done if I had been there.'

"I said: 'Hardin, there is no man on earth that can talk about my children like that without fighting, you cowardly s—— of a b——.'

"Hardin said: 'I am unarmed.'

"I said: 'Go and get your gun. I am armed.'

"Then he said, 'I'll go and get a gun and when I meet you I'll meet you smoking and make you pull like a wolf around the block.'

"Hardin then went into the saloon and began shaking dice with Henry Brown. I met my son John and Capt. Carr and told them I expected trouble when Hardin came out of the saloon. I told my son all that had occurred, but told him not to have anything to do with it, but to keep on his beat. I also notified Capt. Carr that I expected trouble with Har-

142

din. I then sat down on a beer keg in front of the Acme saloon and waited for Hardin to come out. I insisted on the police force keeping out of the trouble because it was a personal matter between Hardin and myself. Hardin had insulted me personally.

"About 11 o'clock Mr. E. L. Shackleford came along and met me on the sidewalk. He said: 'Hello, what are you doing here?'

"Then Shackleford insisted on me going inside and taking a drink, but I said, 'No, I do not want to go in there as Hardin is in there and I am afraid we will have trouble.'

"Shackleford then said: 'Come on and take a drink anyhow, but don't get drunk.' Shackleford led me into the saloon by the arm. Hardin and Brown were shaking dice at the end of the bar next to the door. While we were drinking I noticed that Hardin watched me very closely as we went in. When he thought my eye was off him he made a break for his gun in his hip pocket and I immediately pulled my gun and began shooting. I shot him in the head first as I had been informed that he wore a steel breast plate. As I was about to shoot the second time some one ran against me and I think I missed him, but the other two shots were at his body and I think I hit him both times. My son then ran in and caught me by the arm and said: 'He is dead. Don't shoot any more.'

"I was not drunk at the time, but was crazy mad at the way he had insulted me.

"My son and myself came out of the saloon together and when Justice Howe came I gave my statement to him. My wife was very weak and was prostrated when I got home. I was accompanied home by Deputy Sheriff J. C. Jones. I was not placed in jail, but considered myself under arrest. I am willing to stand any investigation over the matter. I

143

am sorry I had to kill Hardin, but he had threatened mine and my son's life several times and I felt that it had come to that point where either I or he had to die.

(Signed) "JOHN SELMAN"

Frank Patterson, the bartender at the Acme Saloon, testified before the coroner as follows:

"My name is Frank Patterson. I am a bar tender at present at the Acme saloon. This evening about 11 o'clock J. W. Hardin was standing with Henry Brown shaking dice and Mr. Selman walked in at the door and shot him. Mr. G. L. Shackleford was also in the saloon at the time the shooting took place. Mr. Selman said something as he came in at the door. Hardin was standing with his back to Mr. Selman. I did not see him face around before he fell or make any motion. All I saw was that Mr. Selman came in the door, said something and shot and Hardin fell. Don't think Hardin ever spoke. The first shot was in the head.

(Signed) "F. F. PATTERSON"

Mr. E. L. Shackleford testified as follows:

"My name is E. L. Shackleford; am in the general brokerage business. When I came down the street this evening I had understood from some parties that Mr. Hardin had made some threats against Mr. Selman, who had formerly been in my employ and was a friend of mine. I came over to the Acme saloon, where I met Mr. Selman. At the time I met Mr. Selman he was in the saloon with several others and was drinking with them. I told him I had understood there was occasion for him to have trouble, and having heard of the character of the man with whom he would have trouble, I advised him as a friend not to get under the influence of liquor. We walked out on the sidewalk and

144

came back into the saloon, I being some distance ahead of Selman, walking towards the back of the saloon. There I heard shots fired. I can't say who fired the shots, as I did not see it. I did not turn around, but left immedaitely. The room was full of powder smoke, and I could not have seen anything anyhow.

(Signed) "E. L. SHACKLEFORD."

Mr. R. B. Stevens, the proprietor of the Acme saloon, said:

"I was on the street and some one told me there was likely to be trouble at my saloon between Wes Hardin and John Selman, Sr. I came down to the saloon and walked in. Selman was sitting outside the door. Hardin was standing just inside the door at the bar, shaking dice with Henry Brown. I walked on back into the reading room and sat down where I could see the bar. Soon Selman and Shackleford came in and took a drink. I then understood Shackleford to say to Selman: 'Come out, now; you are drinking, and I don't want you to have any trouble.' They when out together. I then supposed Selman had gone away and there would be no trouble. I leaned back against a post and was talking to Shorty Anderson, and could not see the front door, and do not know who came in. When Selman and Shackleford came in they took a drink at the inside of the bar. Hardin and Brown were standing at the end of the bar next the door. I did not see Selman when the shooting took place. When I went into the barroom Hardin was lying on the floor near the door and was dead. I walked to the door and looked out. Selman was standing in front with several others, Capt. Carr among them. When Capt. Carr came into the saloon I asked him to take charge of Hardin's body and keep the crowd out. He said he could

145

not move the body until the crowd viewed it. I saw Carr take two pistols off Hardin's body. One was a white-handled pistol and the other a black-handled one. They were both .41 caliber Colts. The bullet that passed through Hardin's head struck a mirror frame and glanced off and fell in front of the bar at the lower end. In the floor where Hardin fell are three bullet holes in triangular shape about a span across. They range straight through the floor."

Henry Brown testified as follows:

"My name is H. S. Brown. I am in the grocery business in El Paso with Mr. Lambert. I dropped into the Acme saloon last night a little before 11 o'clock and met Mr. Hardin and several other parties in there, and Mr. Hardin offered to shake with me. I agreed, and shook first; he shook back, and said he'd bet me a quarter on the side he could beat me. We had our quarters up and he and I were shaking dice. I heard a shot fired, and Mr. Hardin fell at my feet at my left side. I heard three or four shots fired. I then left, went out the back door, and don't know what occurred afterwards. When the shot was fired Mr. Hardin was against the bar, facing it, as near as I can say, and his back was towards the direction the shot came from. I did not see him make any effort to get his six-shooter. The last words he spoke before the first shot was fired were, 'Four sixes to beat,' and they were addressed to me. For a moment or two before this he had not spoken to anyone but me, to the best of my recollection. I had not the slightest idea that anyone was quarreling there from anything I heard.

(Signed) "H. S. BROWN"

The following evidence was given Justice Howe this afternoon by the three physicians whose names are signed thereto:

146

"We, the undersigned, practicing physicians, hereby certify that we have examined the gunshot wounds on the person of the deceased, John Wesley Hardin, and it is our opinion that the wound causing death was caused by a bullet; that the bullet entered near the base of the skull posteriorly and came out at the upper corner of the left eye.

(Signed)

"S. G. SHERARD,

"W. N. VILAS,

"ALWARD WHITE"

The wounds on Hardin's body were on the back of the head, coming out just over the left eye. Another shot in the right breast, just missing the nipple, and another through the right arm. The body was embalmed by Undertaker Powell and will be interred at Concordia at 4 P.M.

THE KILLING OF SELMAN

—

HARDIN'S SLAYER DID NOT long survive his victim. The following newspaper account details the manner of his death at the hands of ex-Sheriff George Scarborough, of Jones County, on the 5th of April, 1896:

El Paso, Texas—John Selman, the victor of not less than twenty shooting affrays in Texas, the exterminator of "bad men" and the slayer of John Wesley Hardin, is dying tonight with a bullet hole through his body. About three months ago Selman and United States Deputy Marshal Geo. Scarborough had a quarrel over a game of cards, since which occurrence the relations between them have not been cordial. This morning at 4 o'clock they met in the Wigwam saloon and both were drinking. Scarborough says that Selman said, "Come, I want to see you," and that the two men walked into an alley beside the saloon, and Selman, whose son is in Juárez, Mexico, in jail on a charge of abducting a young lady from there to this side, said to Scarborough: "I want you to come over the river with me this morning. We must get that boy out of jail."

Scarborough expressed his willingness to go with Selman, but stated that no bad breaks must be made in Juárez. Scarborough says that Selman then reached for his pistol, with the remark, "I believe I will kill you." Scarborough pulled his gun and began shooting. At the second shot Selman fell, and Scarborough fired two more shots as Selman attempted to rise. When Selman was searched no pistol could be found on him or anywhere around him. He says he had a pistol, but that it was taken from him after he fell and before the police reached him. Scarborough's first shot hit Selman in the neck. The next two shots also took effect, one through the left leg just above the knee and the other entering the right side just under the lower rib. A fourth wound in the right hip is supposed to have been caused by Selman's pistol going off prematurely, as the ball ranged downward. Scarborough is about 38 years old. He was born in Louisiana and was raised in Texas, and for several years was sheriff of Jones County. Selman was raised on the Colorado River in Texas. He was about 58 years old and has lived a stormy life. When not drinking he was as gentle as a child, but he did not know what fear was, and has killed not less than twenty outlaws. He was a dead shot and quick with his gun. He was an old officer in the service. Some years ago he fought a band of cattle thieves in Donna Anna County, New Mexico, killing two and capturing the others, four in all. He killed Bass Outlaw, a deputy United States Marshal, in El Paso a few years ago.